Contents

T0345723

GoGetter Tests

This booklet contains a complete tests package for *GoGetter* 1. All of the tests are in photocopiable format. Audio for the listening tasks is available for downloading from MyEnglishLab.

Assessment of learning or Assessment for learning?

GoGetter offers a variety of tests which enable the teacher to monitor students' progress both at acquiring the new language and developing language skills. Any test can be used either as an assessment of learning or an assessment for learning. Assessment of learning usually takes place after the learning has happened and provides information about what students have achieved by giving a mark or a grade. You can also use a test as an assessment for learning by providing specific feedback on students' strengths and weaknesses, and suggestions for improvement as part of the on-going learning process. A combination of both types of assessment can be a powerful tool for helping your students to learn.

It is very important to make sure students understand the tasks in every test and explain them if necessary. Also, it is very useful for students to receive constructive feedback and be advised how they can improve.

Versions of tests

Most tests have two versions: A and B. Versions A and B feature the same task types and are designed to have the same level of difficulty. However, the test items in each version are usually different or the sequence in which they occur differs. In the listening tasks, the test items are different but the audio is the same for both A and B versions, which makes it easy to administer a test.

You can use the tests that have two versions in two ways:

- give half the students in the class the A version and the other half the B version – this will help to deter students from cheating.
- give all students in the class the A version. You can then use the B version for students who missed the test or would like to retake it. Students who need a little more work on the unit objectives can use version B as remedial material.

Types of tests

Placement Test

The *GoGetter 1* Placement Test has been designed to help you decide which level of the *GoGetter* series, level 1 or level 2, is best suited to your students. If students score:

- 0–25 points (0–50%), we suggest they start at level 1.
- 26–37 points (51–74%), you might consider an additional oral interview to decide whether level 1 or level 2 (the latter with some remedial work) would be more appropriate.
- 38–50 points (75+%), we suggest they start at level 2.

Vocabulary Checks

There are eight Vocabulary Checks. They test the key vocabulary sets taught in units 1–8 of the Students' Book. Each Vocabulary Check comprises three exercises. A Vocabulary Check can be administered upon completing all lessons with vocabulary input in a unit. Alternatively, it can be cut up into three mini-tests and administered after completing work on the relevant vocabulary set.

Grammar Checks

There are eight Grammar Checks. They test the grammar taught in lessons 2 and 3 of units 1–8 of the Students' Book. Each Grammar Check comprises three exercises. A Grammar Check can be administered upon completing lesson 3 of a unit. Alternatively, it can be cut up into two mini-tests and administered after completing work on the relevant grammar point.

Language Tests

There are nine Language Tests. They test the vocabulary, grammar and language for communication taught in the *Get started!* unit and units 1–8 of the Students' Book. The tests can be administered upon completing each unit.

Skills Tests

There are four Skills Tests. Each exploits the language taught in two successive units of the Students' Book. The Skills Tests check students' progress using the following skills-based tasks: Listening, Communication, Reading and Writing. In each test one of the listening tasks and the communication task mirror the exam-style tasks used in the relevant Skills Revision section in the Students' Book. The tests can be administered upon completing units 2, 4, 6 and 8.

Mid-Year Test and End-of-Year Test

The Mid-Year Test and the End-of-Year Test have the same structure and consist of two parts. The first part, Exercises 1–6, tests the vocabulary and grammar taught in the relevant units of the Students' Book. The second part, Exercises 7–9, is skills-based and comprises Listening, Communication and Reading. The Mid-Year Test should be administered after completing the first four units of the Students' Book, and the End-of-Year Test – after all units have been completed.

Exam Tests

There are two Exam Tests. Exam Test 1–4 should be used after completing the first four units of the Students' Book including *Skills Revision*. Exam Test 5–8 should be administered after units 5–8 have been completed. The two tests mirror the Exam Practice section of the *GoGetter 1 Workbook* and comprise two sections: Reading & Writing and Listening & Communication. These tests provide the opportunity to check students' progress and proficiency through typical exam tasks similar to those in *Pearson Test of English for Young Learners* and *Cambridge English: Young Learners of English Tests* (adapted to suit this level and age group).

Speaking Tasks

There are four sets of Speaking Tasks, each enabling you to test the material from two successive units. Each set has visual material for the student and notes for the teacher at the bottom of the page, which should be cut off along the dotted line. There are two tasks in the notes for the teacher:

- Task 1: elicitation of the vocabulary illustrated,
- Task 2: asking and answering personalised questions related to both the picture and the student's experience.

The student should respond using structures and vocabulary from the relevant units.

The Speaking Tasks can complement the respective Skills Tests, Mid-Year Test and End-of-Year Test or be administered separately. The following marking criteria and evaluation scales will help you mark consistently and give students meaningful feedback.

Marking criteria

- 0–5 points for the range of language used (structures and vocabulary). See the list of target structures and vocabulary for each Speaking Task in the notes for the teacher.
- 0–5 points for accuracy of expression
- 0–5 points for fluency
- 0–5 points for pronunciation

Evaluation scales	Language range	Accuracy	Fluency	Pronunciation
Excellent 18–20 points	The student commands a full range of the vocabulary and grammar taught and uses it appropriately.	The student makes no or very few mistakes.	The student speaks fluently, with no hesitation. He/She can use full sentences. Students should not be penalised for using single words or phrases where appropriate.	The student's pronunciation is clear and accurate.
Good 15–17 points	The student commands a good range of the vocabulary and grammar taught.	The student makes mistakes occasionally.	The student speaks fluently, with little hesitation. He/She can use full sentences. Students should not be penalised for using single words or phrases where appropriate.	The student's pronunciation is clear and accurate most of the time.
Satisfactory 10–14 points	The student can use some of the basic vocabulary and grammar taught.	The student makes mistakes but these do not prevent communication.	The student speaks with some hesitation because he/she is trying to think of the right words. He/She answers using full sentences some of the time but clearly prefers using phrases.	The student's pronunciation is clear on the whole; occasional poor pronunciation does not prevent communication.
Unsatisfactory 6–9 points	The student can use very little vocabulary and grammar.	The student makes a lot of mistakes which hinder good communication. He/She is able to communicate successfully at least once.	The student hesitates frequently because he/she cannot think of the right words. He/She answers using mainly phrases or single words.	The student's pronunciation is poor and makes communication difficult.
Very poor 0–5 points	The student gives no answer or knows only a few basic words.	The student is unable to communicate or gives inaccurate answers that prevent communication.	The student cannot think of the right words and says very little.	The student gives no answer or can pronounce fairly correctly only a few words.

Writing Tasks

There are eight Writing Tasks corresponding to Units 1–8 in the Students' Book. You can use the tasks as in-class writing tests or assign them as homework.

Each writing task contains a topic, several questions that students are asked to refer to in their works and a word limit. Tasks for units 1–5 have a 40–50-word limit, whereas those for units 6–8 have a 40–70-word limit.

The following marking criteria and evaluation scales are provided to help you mark consistently and to give students meaningful feedback.

Marking criteria

- 0–5 points for content. Award 5 marks if the student refers to at least 5 questions / gives 5 different pieces of information connected with the topic.
- 1 point for not going under or over the word limit.
- 2 points for accuracy of expression.
- 2 points for the range of language used. See the Marking check lists and model texts for each writing task on page 95 of this booklet.

Evaluation scales

Excellent:	9–10 points
Good:	7–8 points
Satisfactory:	5–6 points
Unsatisfactory:	3–4 points
Very poor:	0–2 points

Tests on MyEnglishLab

Visit www.MyEnglishLab.com to access the following:

- online versions of Skills tests, Mid-Year Test and End-of-Year Test, which can be assigned to your students and automatically checked,
- *GoGetter Tests* in PDF and editable format, and audio for tests,
- PDF versions of *GoGetter Tests* adjusted to the needs of dyslectic students.

Use the Teacher Access Code to unlock the teacher content on MyEnglishLab. You will find the code and registration details in *GoGetter* Teacher's Book.

Placement Test A

name ______________________ class ________

Vocabulary

1 Circle the odd one out.

0	black	green	red	[dog]
1	mother	family	father	uncle
2	China	British	Italian	French
3	book	pen	lesson	rubber
4	shoes	dress	jeans	skateboard
5	kitchen	classroom	bathroom	living room

☐ / [5]

2 Match the words from the box to the pictures. There is one extra word.

feet giraffe legs monkey rabbit ~~snake~~ teeth

0 *snake*

1 ____________

2 ____________

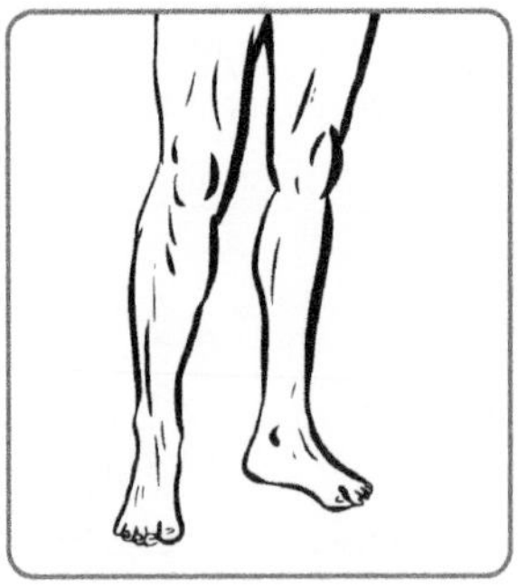

3 ____________

4 ____________

5 ____________

☐ / [5]

3 Circle the correct word.

0 I can *fly* / [*ride*] / *run* a bike.
1 I *play* / *make* / *go* swimming in the summer.
2 I *act* / *drink* / *eat* a lot of water.
3 I *do* / *make* / *go* my homework every afternoon.
4 I *look* / *listen* / *go* to music in the evening.
5 I *do* / *make* / *have* a shower before breakfast.

☐ / [5]

4 Complete the text with the words in the box. There is one extra word.

~~blond~~ clever console cute dangerous draw hamster

HOME | ABOUT ME | CONTACT

Mary Morris is my best friend. Her hair is [0] *blond* and her eyes are brown. She's very talented. She can [1] ____________ great pictures and she can sing well. She's [2] ____________ too, and she gets good marks at school. Her favourite thing is her games [3] ____________. She also loves her pet [4] ____________. Its name is Cupcake and it's very [5] ____________!

☐ / [5]

Grammar

5 Circle the correct word.

0 Alex and Mark *am* / *is* / [*are*] my cousins.
1 How old *am* / *is* / *are* your brother?
2 Look at Wanda and Kylie! *They* / *There* / *Their* hair is red.
3 This cat is black but *the* / *that* / *those* cats are white.
4 *Am I* / *I am* / *I'm* clever and nice?
5 Tom is eleven and *her* / *his* / *its* sister is eight.

☐ / [5]

© Pearson Education Limited 2017 PHOTOCOPIABLE

Placement Test A

name _____ class _____

6 Match questions 1–5 with answers a–e.

0 Are there three lions in the zoo? [f]
1 Can Elaine tell funny jokes? [ ]
2 Have you and Martha got a big house? [ ]
3 Does the tiger like eating fruit? [ ]
4 Has your best friend got a lot of comics? [ ]
5 Do the children get up early on Saturdays? [ ]

a No, he hasn't.   d Yes, they do.
b Yes, she can.   e Yes, we have.
c No, it doesn't.   f No, there aren't.

[ ] / [5]

7 Put the words in the correct order to make sentences and questions.

0 on / there / a carpet / is / the floor ?
   Is there a carpet on the floor?

1 the museum / can / do / at / we / what / ?
   _____

2 go / on / my parents / don't / Sundays / work / to / .
   _____

3 there / trees / the garden / any / in / aren't / .
   _____

4 where / live / do / your aunt and uncle / ?
   _____

5 TV / in / Susan / watches / the evening / always / .
   _____

[ ] / [5]

8 Complete the text. Choose the correct answer.

My granny ⁰____ in the country and I love ¹____ to her house. There are wild animals in her garden and I watch ²____ from the living room window. Granny is eighty years old and she ³____ a lot of jobs in the house. I always help ⁴____ when I'm in the country. ⁵____ you help your grandparents?

0 **a** live	(**b**) lives	**c** living
1 **a** go	**b** goes	**c** going
2 **a** it	**b** them	**c** him
3 **a** not do	**b** don't do	**c** can't do
4 **a** her	**b** him	**c** us
5 **a** Do	**b** Is	**c** Have

[ ] / [5]

Communication

9 Complete the dialogues. Choose the correct answer.

0 **A:** Hello, Jimmy. Nice to meet you.
   B: a I'm fine, thanks.
   (**b**) Nice to meet you too.
   c I like it too.

1 **A:** What's your favourite sport?
   B: a I love football.
   b It's Ronaldo.
   c Making cakes.

2 **A:** Would you like a sandwich?
   B: a Yes, I do.
   b It's OK.
   c No, thank you.

3 **A:** Sorry, my mistake.
   B: a You aren't.
   b You too.
   c No problem.

4 **A:** Let's go cycling.
   B: a Great idea.
   b No, I don't.
   c I'm sure.

5 **A:** What time is it?
   B: a At five.
   b Quarter past two.
   c In the summer.

[ ] / [5]

10 Complete the dialogues with the words in the box.

fine   have   here   idea   let   ~~spell~~

A: How do you ⁰_spell_ 'wardrobe'?
B: W – A – R – D – R – O – B – E.

A: Where's the bathroom, please?
B: ¹_____ me show you.

A: Are you OK?
B: I'm ²_____.

A: We can go to the park this afternoon.
B: It's not a good ³_____.

A: Can I ⁴_____ two tickets to the museum, please?
B: ⁵_____ you are.

[ ] / [5]

Vocabulary [ ] / [20]	Communication [ ] / [10]
Grammar [ ] / [20]	**Your total score** [ ] / [50]

Placement Test B

name _____   class _____

Vocabulary

1 Circle the odd one out.

0 black	green	red	~~dog~~
1 aunt	family	brother	grandad
2 Spain	Italian	Chinese	Polish
3 pencil	floor	ruler	rubber
4 trousers	jacket	skateboard	shoes
5 bathroom	kitchen	bedroom	classroom

☐ / ⑤

2 Match the words from the box to the pictures. There is one extra word.

> feet giraffe legs monkey rabbit ~~snake~~
> teeth

0 *snake*

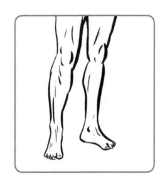

1 _____

2 _____

3 _____

4 _____

5 _____

☐ / ⑤

3 Circle the correct word.

0 I can *fly / ride / run* a bike.

1 I *do / go / make* my homework every afternoon.

2 I *make / have / write* Art lessons at school.

3 I *drink / eat / act* fruit and vegetables.

4 I *play / make / go* skiing in the winter.

5 I *watch / listen / have* TV in the evening.

☐ / ⑤

4 Complete the text with the words in the box. There is one extra word.

> clever cute dangerous ~~dark~~ hamster
> mountain play

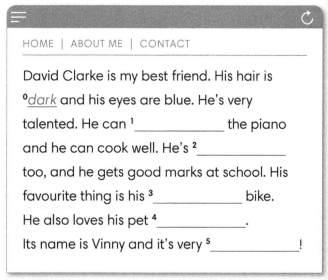

HOME | ABOUT ME | CONTACT

David Clarke is my best friend. His hair is
⁰*dark* and his eyes are blue. He's very
talented. He can ¹_____ the piano
and he can cook well. He's ²_____
too, and he gets good marks at school. His
favourite thing is his ³_____ bike.
He also loves his pet ⁴_____.
Its name is Vinny and it's very ⁵_____!

☐ / ⑤

Grammar

5 Circle the correct word.

0 Alex and Mark *am / is / are* my cousins.

1 Where *am / is / are* the television?

2 These hoodies are blue but *the / those / that* hoodie is black.

3 Jules and Robbie have got red hair and *there / their / they* eyes are green.

4 Helen is twelve and *her / his / its* brother is nine.

5 *I am / Am I / I'm* a good student?

☐ / ⑤

8

Placement Test B

name ______________________ class ______

6 Match questions 1–5 with answers a–e.

0 Are there three lions in the zoo? [f]
1 Does the rabbit like eating plants? ☐
2 Do the children go to bed early on Mondays? ☐
3 Can Harry play the piano? ☐
4 Has your cousin got a mobile phone? ☐
5 Have you and Sally got a pet dog? ☐

a No, she hasn't.
b Yes, they do.
c No, he can't.
d Yes, we have.
e Yes, it does.
f No, there aren't.

☐ / [5]

7 Put the words in the correct order to make sentences and questions.

0 on / there / a carpet / is / the floor ?
Is there a carpet on the floor?
1 we / do / at / can / what / the museum / ?
____
2 the lesson / when / finish / does / ?
____
3 go / on / Saturdays / my friends / don't / to / school / .
____
4 in / never / the evening / TV / watches / Luke / .
____
5 aren't / any / on / cushions / there / the sofa / .
____

☐ / [5]

8 Complete the text. Choose the correct answer.

My grandad ⁰____ in the country. There are lots of birds in his garden and I watch ¹____ from the living room window. I like ²____ at all the flowers too. Grandad is eighty years old and he ³____ do a lot of jobs in the house. Mum and I always help ⁴____ when we're in the country. ⁵____ you help your grandparents?

0	**a** live	[b] lives	**c** living
1	**a** it	**b** them	**c** her
2	**a** look	**b** looks	**c** looking
3	**a** can't	**b** not	**c** don't
4	**a** us	**b** her	**c** him
5	**a** Do	**b** Does	**c** Is

☐ / [5]

Communication

9 Complete the dialogues. Choose the correct answer.

0 **A:** Hello, Jimmy. Nice to meet you.
B: a I'm fine, thanks.
[b] Nice to meet you too.
c I like it too.

1 **A:** Would you like some water?
B: a No, I don't.
b Yes, please.
c It's OK.

2 **A:** Let's go windsurfing.
B: a I'm sure.
b Yes, I can.
c Great idea.

3 **A:** Who is your favourite actor?
B: a Football.
b Emma Watson.
c Beauty and the Beast.

4 **A:** Sorry about that!
B: a That's all right.
b Yes, it is.
c You're OK.

5 **A:** What's the weather like?
B: a It's nine o'clock.
b It's cloudy.
c In the winter.

☐ / [5]

10 Complete the dialogues with the words in the box.

fine here idea please show ~~spell~~

A: How do you ⁰*spell* 'wardrobe'?
B: W – A – R – D – R – O – B – E.

A: We can go to the museum this afternoon.
B: It's not a good ¹__________.

A: Where's the bathroom?
B: Let me ²__________ you.

A: Can I have four tickets to the zoo, ³__________?
B: ⁴__________ you are.

A: Are you OK?
B: Yes, I'm ⁵__________.

☐ / [5]

Vocabulary	☐ / [20]	Communication	☐ / [10]
Grammar	☐ / [20]	**Your total score**	☐ / [50]

1 Vocabulary Check A

name class

1.1 Family

A

1 **Look at the family tree. Complete the text with the words in the box.**

aunt brother cousin daughter father grandfather grandmother ~~mother~~ sister son uncle

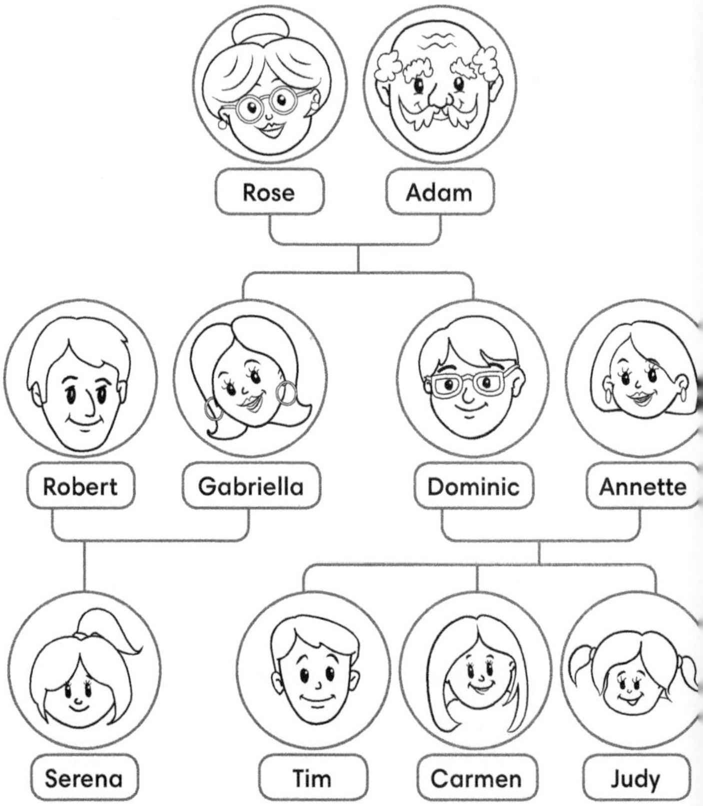

Hi! I'm Carmen. This is my family tree. My 0*mother* and 1__________ are Annette and Dominic. Rose is my 2__________ and Adam is my 3__________. Dominic is Adam's 4__________ and Gabriella is Adam's 5__________. Robert is my 6__________ and Gabriella is my 7__________. Tim is my 8__________ and Judy is my 9__________. Serena is my 10__________.

☐ / [10]

name class

1.3 Countries and nationalities

A

2 **Complete the sentences. Write countries or nationalities.**

0 I'm from the UK. I'm **B** *r i t i s h*.
1 Claude is from **F** _ _ _ _ _. He's French.
2 Li and Chen are from China. They're **C** _ _ _ _ _ _ _.
3 Dorota is from **P** _ _ _ _ _. She's Polish.
4 You're from the USA. You're **A** _ _ _ _ _ _ _ _.
5 Carlo is from **I** _ _ _ _. He's Italian.

☐ / [5]

name class

1.5 Places

A

3 **Circle the correct word.**

0 I'm (at) / *in* / *on* home.
1 The dog is *at* / *in* / *on* the garden.
2 My friends are *at* / *in* / *on* a party.
3 You aren't *at* / *to* / *on* school today.
4 Alice's sister isn't here. She's *at* / *in* / *on* holiday.
5 My brothers and I are *to* / *in* / *on* the park.

☐ / [5]

Your total score ☐ / [20]

1 Vocabulary Check B

name _____   class _____

1.1 Family   A

1 Look at the family tree. Complete the text with the words in the box.

> aunt brother cousin daughter father
> grandfather grandmother ~~mother~~ sister
> son uncle

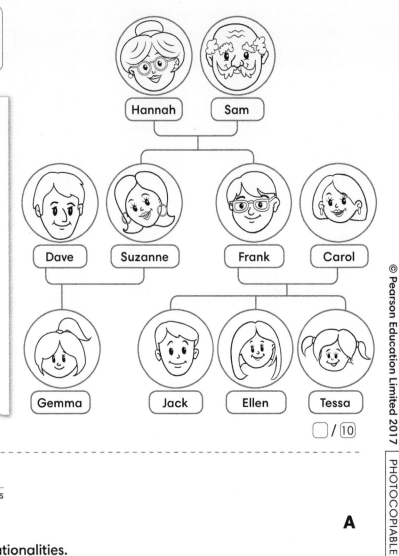

Hi! I'm Ellen. This is my family tree.

My ⁰*mother* and ¹_____ are Carol and

Frank. Tessa is my ²_____ and Jack is

my ³_____. Suzanne is my ⁴_____

and Dave is my ⁵_____.

Sam is my ⁶_____ and Hannah is

my ⁷_____. Suzanne's ⁸_____ is

Gemma. Jack is Frank's ⁹_____.

Gemma is Tessa's ¹⁰_____.

☐ / ⑩

- -

name _____   class _____

1.3 Countries and nationalities   A

2 Complete the sentences. Write countries or nationalities.

0 I'm from the UK. I'm **B** *r i t i s h*.

1 Felipe is from **S** _ _ _ _. He's Spanish.

2 Jake and Lee are from the USA.
  They're **A** _ _ _ _ _ _ _.

3 Stefania is from **I** _ _ _ _. She's Italian.

4 You're from Poland. You're **P** _ _ _ _ _.

5 Li is from **C** _ _ _ _. He's Chinese.

☐ / ⑤

- -

name _____   class _____

1.5 Places   A

3 Circle the correct word.

0 I'm ⓐt / in / on home.

1 Tina isn't here. She's *at / in / on* holiday.

2 The students aren't *at / to / on* school.

3 The girls are is *to / in / on* the park.

4 We are *at / in / on* a party.

5 Are you *at / in / on* the garden?

☐ / ⑤

Your total score ☐ / ⑳   **11**

2 Vocabulary Check A

name class

2.1 Clothes A

1 Look at the picture and write the words. There is one extra word.

cap coat dress hoodie jacket
jeans jumper shirt skirt trainers
trousers ~~T-shirt~~

0 *T-shirt*
1 ______
2 ______
3 ______
4 ______
5 ______
6 ______
7 ______
8 ______
9 ______
10 ______

/ [10]

name class

2.2 Adjectives A

2 Circle the correct word.

0 Jim's cat isn't white! Look, it's *green* / *purple* / *black*!
1 These shoes aren't big. They're *new* / *short* / *small*.
2 Joanna's dress is old. It isn't *new* / *boring* / *long*.
3 The trousers are long. They aren't *cool* / *short* / *big*.
4 The hoodie isn't cool. It's *big* / *boring* / *short*.
5 No, this cap is too small. Look at that *long* / *big* / *short* cap over there!

/ [5]

name class

2.5 My things A

3 Complete the words.

0 Ewa's favourite thing is her **l** *a p t o p* computer.
1 Jack's favourite thing is his **m** _ _ _ _ _ phone.
2 Marco's favourite thing is his skate**b** _ _ _ _.
3 Lucy's favourite thing is her **m** _ _ _ _ _ _ _ bike.
4 Theo's favourite thing is his games **c** _ _ _ _ _ _.
5 Gina's favourite thing is her **b** _ _ _pack.

/ [5]

Your total score / [20]

2 Vocabulary Check B

name class

2.1 Clothes B

1 Look at the picture and write the words. There is one extra word.

boots cap coat dress hoodie
jacket jeans jumper shirt shoes
skirt ~~T-shirt~~

0 *T-shirt*
1 ________
2 ________
3 ________
4 ________
5 ________
6 ________
7 ________
8 ________
9 ________
10 ________

☐ / [10]

name class

2.2 Adjectives B

2 Circle the correct word.

0 Jim's cat isn't white! Look, it's *green / purple / black*!
1 These shoes aren't big. They're *new / short / small*.
2 Those jeans aren't boring. They're *old / long / cool*.
3 The coat isn't long. It's *short / small / new*.
4 No, that jacket is too small. Look at this *long / short / big jacket* here!
5 My jumper is new. It isn't *short / old / cool*.

☐ / [5]

name class

2.5 My things B

3 Complete the words.

0 Ewa's favourite thing is her **l** *a p t o p* computer.
1 Olivia's favourite thing is her **m** _ _ _ _ _ _ _ _ bike.
2 Harry's favourite thing is his games **c** _ _ _ _ _ _.
3 Luke's favourite thing is his back**p** _ _ _.
4 Jack's favourite thing is his **m** _ _ _ _ _ phone.
5 Zac's favourite thing is his **s** _ _ _ _board.

☐ / [5]

Your total score ☐ / [20]

name _____ class _____

3.1 In the house

A

1 Look at the picture. Write the words.

0 b <u>e d r o o</u> m
1 w _ _ _ _ _ _ e
2 d _ _ r
3 b _ _ _
4 l _ _ _ _ g r _ _ m
5 s _ _ a
6 t _ _ _ e
7 f _ _ _ _ e
8 c _ _ _ _ s
9 g _ _ _ _ e
10 g _ _ _ _ n

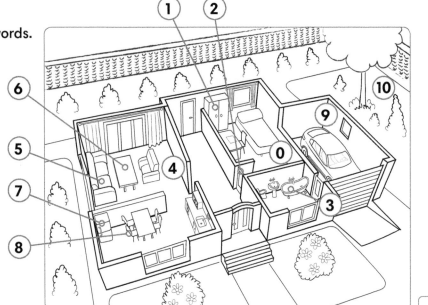

☐ / ⑩

---

name _____ class _____

3.2 Prepositions of place

A

2 Match pictures 1–5 with sentences a–e.

a It's behind the box.
b It's in front of the box.
c It's next to the box.
d It's on the box.
e It's under the box.
f It's in the box.

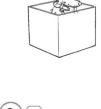

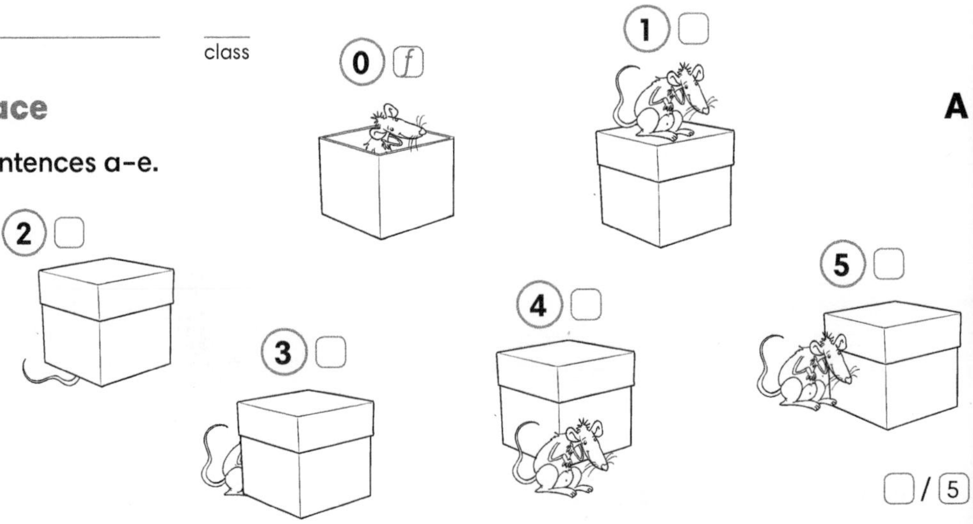

0 [f]
1 ☐
2 ☐
3 ☐
4 ☐
5 ☐

☐ / ⑤

---

name _____ class _____

3.4 Household objects

A

3 Look at the pictures. Write the words.

0 a <u>t e l e v i s i o n</u>
1 a _ _ _ _ _ _ _ 
2 a _ _ _ _ _ _
3 a _ _ _ _ 
4 a _ _ _ _ _ _ _
5 a _ _ _ _ _ _

☐ / ⑤

Your total score ☐ / ⑳

3 Vocabulary Check B

name ______________________ class ______

3.1 In the house

B

1 Look at the picture. Write the words.

0 b e d r o o m
1 d _ _ k
2 c _ _ _ r
3 w _ _ _ _ w
4 b _ _ _ _ _ _ _ m
5 a _ _ _ _ _ _ _ r
6 t _ _ _ e
7 f _ _ _ r
8 w _ _ l
9 k _ _ _ _ _ n
10 g _ _ _ _ e

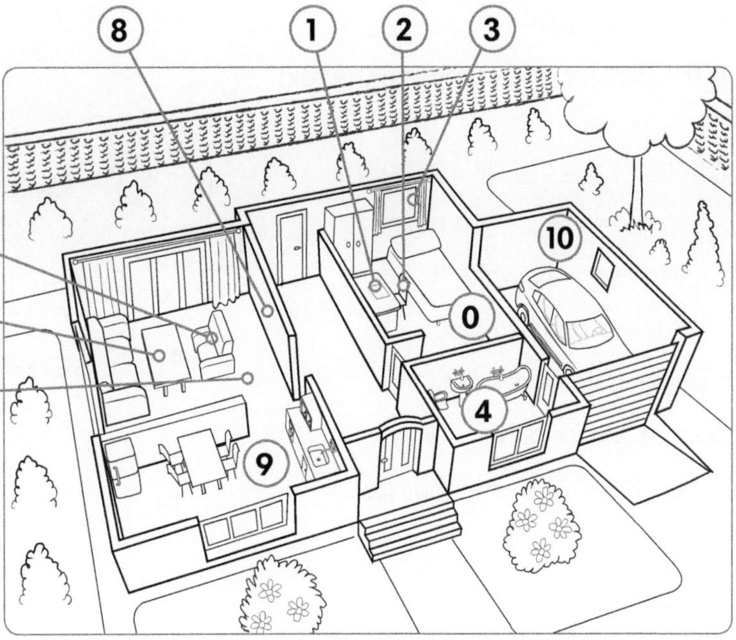

☐ / 10

---

name ______________________ class ______

3.2 Prepositions of place

B

2 Match pictures 1–5 with sentences a–e.

a It's on the box.
b It's in front of the box.
c It's behind the box.
d It's next to the box.
e It's under the box.
f It's in the box.

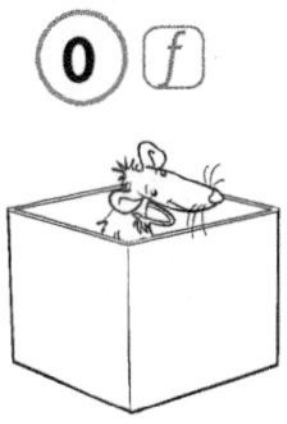
0 f

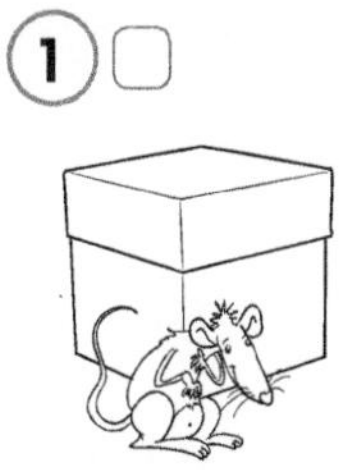
1 ☐

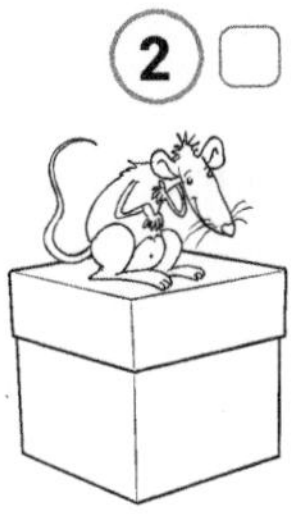
2 ☐

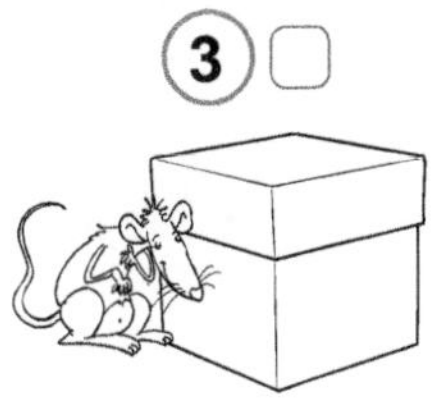
3 ☐

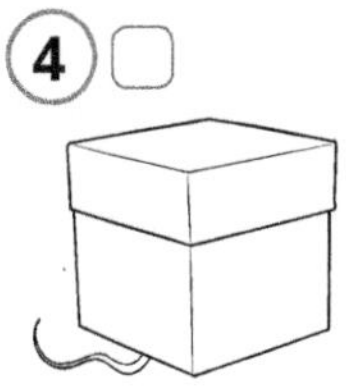
4 ☐

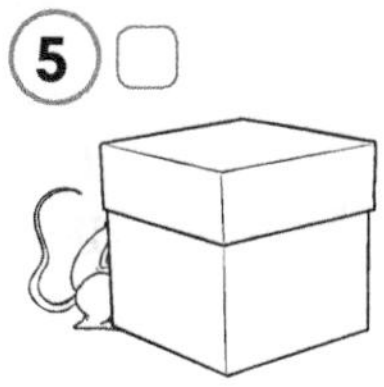
5 ☐

☐ / 5

---

name ______________________ class ______

3.4 Household objects

B

3 Look at the pictures. Write the words.

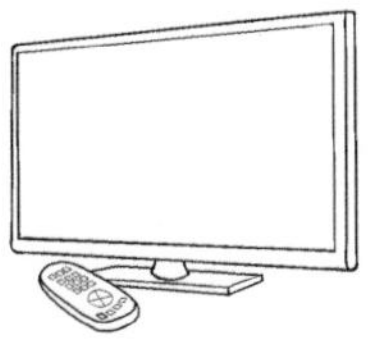
0 a t e l e v i s i o n

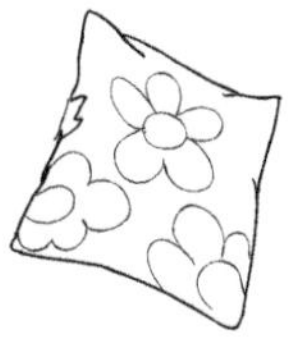
1 a _ _ _ _ _ _ _

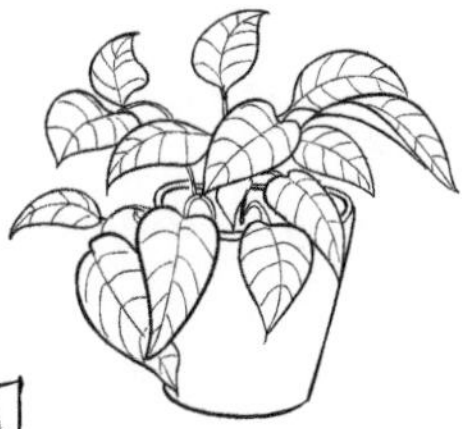
2 a _ _ _ _ _

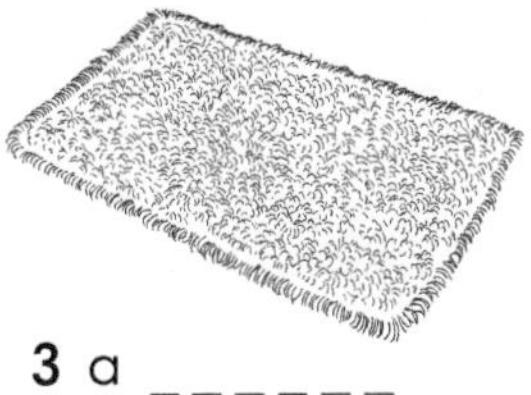
3 a _ _ _ _ _ _

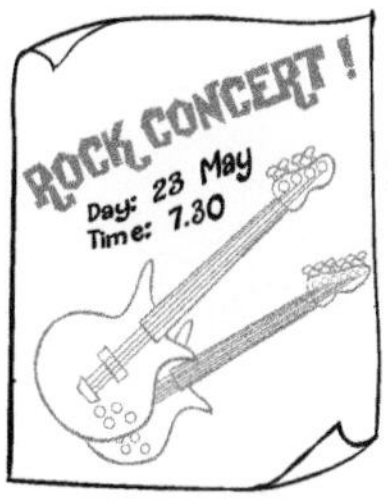

4 a _ _ _ _ _ _

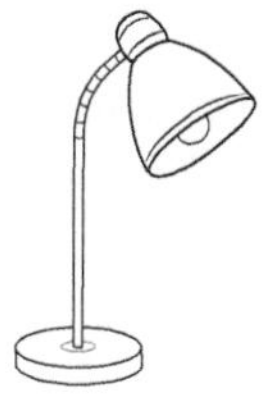
5 a _ _ _ _

☐ / 5

Your total score ☐ / 20

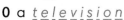

4 Vocabulary Check A

name ______________________ class ______

4.1 Face and hair

1 Look at the picture and complete the text.

Look at Bonzo's 0f *a c e*! He's got big 1e _ _ _, big brown 2e _ _ _, a big red 3m _ _ _ _ and very big white 4t _ _ _ _! His 5n _ _ _ is red and he's got 6c _ _ _ y, green hair. His sister, Glorinda, has got long, 7w _ _ y 8bl _ _ _ hair. Bonzo's brother has got 9s _ _ _ _ _ _ _ t, 10d _ _ k hair.

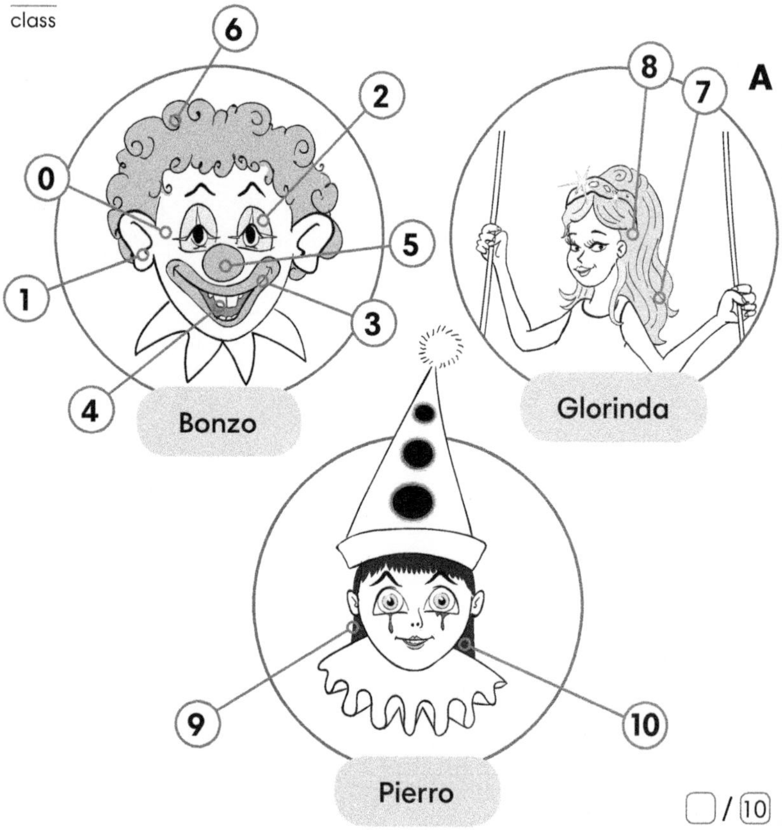

6
2
8
7
A
0
5
1
3
4
Bonzo
Glorinda
9
10
Pierro

☐ / 10

name ______________________ class ______

4.2 Parts of the body

A

2 Find the parts of the body. Then write the words in the correct group.

Your 0*body*:
- head, 1 ______________
- leg, 2 ______________, 3 ______________
- arm, 4 ______________, 5 ______________

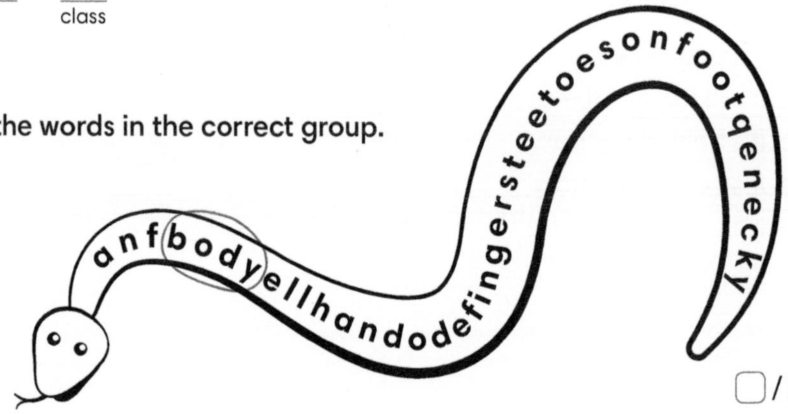

anfbodyellhandodefingersteetoesonfootqenecky

☐ / 5

name ______________________ class ______

4.4 Personality adjectives

A

3 Complete the dialogues with the answers in the box.

You're helpful. You're funny. ~~You're sporty~~. You're clever. You're friendly. You're nice.

0 **A:** I love golf and football.
B: *You're sporty*.

1 **A:** I've got a lovely present for my best friend.
B: ______________________

2 **A:** I've got good marks at school.
B: ______________________

3 **A:** I help my brother with his homework.
B: ______________________

4 **A:** I speak to everyone.
B: ______________________

5 **A:** I tell great jokes.
B: ______________________

☐ / 5

Your total score ☐ / 20

name ____________________ class ____

4.1 Face and hair

B

1 Look at the picture and complete the text.

Look at Pierro's **⁰f** *a c e*! He's got big blue **¹e** _ _ _ and **²s** _ _ _ _ _ _ _ **t**, **³d** _ _ **k** hair. His **⁴n** _ _ _, **⁵e** _ _ _ and **⁶m** _ _ _ _ are small and his **⁷t** _ _ _ _ are small and white. His brother, Bonzo, has got **⁸c** _ _ _ _, green hair but his sister, Glorinda, has got long, **⁹w** _ _ **y** **¹⁰bl** _ _ _ hair.

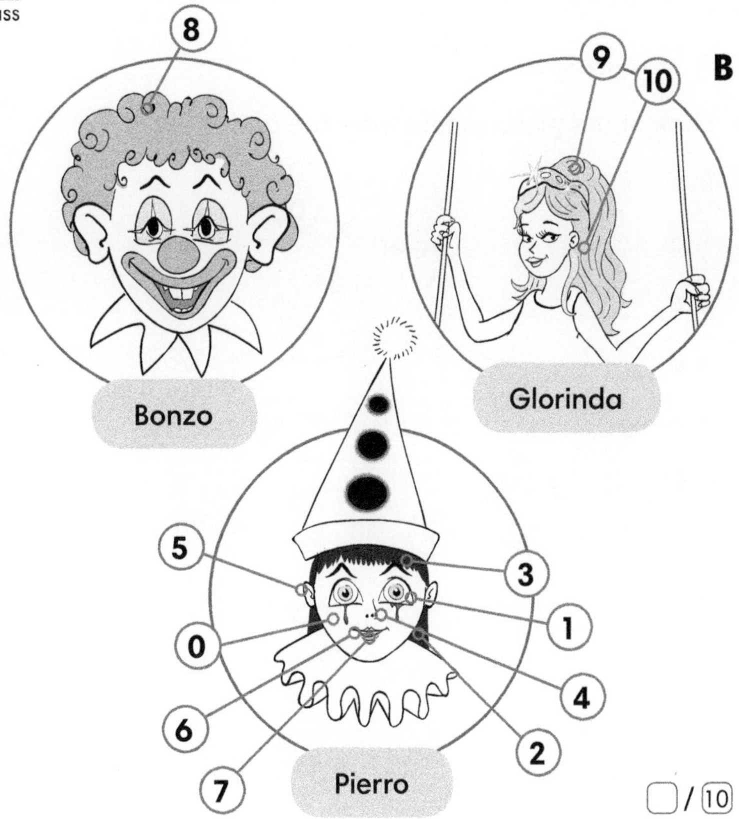

☐ / 10

name ____________________ class ____

4.2 Parts of the body

B

2 Find the parts of the body. Then write the words in the correct group.

Your ⁰*body*:

- ¹__________, hand, ²__________
- neck, ³__________
- ⁴__________, foot, ⁵__________

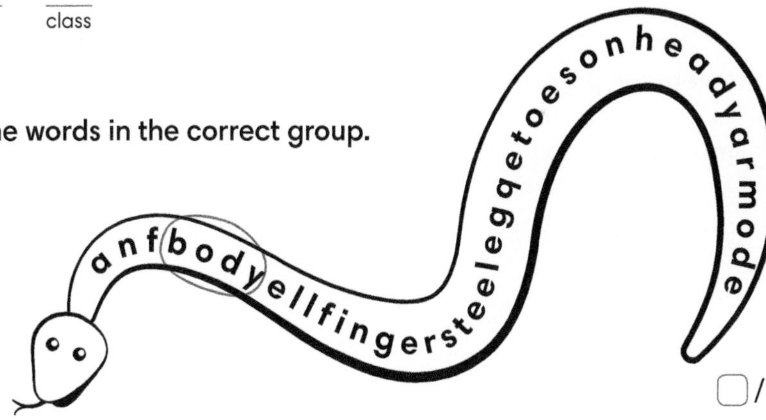

☐ / 5

name ____________________ class ____

4.4 Personality adjectives

B

3 Complete the dialogues with the answers in the box.

You're helpful. You're funny. ~~You're sporty~~. You're clever. You're friendly. You're nice.

0 A: I love golf and football.
B: *You're sporty*.

1 A: I've got great marks at school.
B: ______________________________

2 A: I speak to everyone.
B: ______________________________

3 A: I know very good jokes.
B: ______________________________

4 A: I've got a lovely present for my mum.
B: ______________________________

5 A: I help my friend with her homework.
B: ______________________________

☐ / 5

Your total score ☐ / 20

© Pearson Education Limited 2017 PHOTOCOPIABLE

name ______________________ class ______

5.1 Action verbs

A

1 Look at the pictures and write the action verbs.

0 s *i t*
1 d _ _ _
2 d _ _ _
3 s _ _ _
4 a _ _
5 f _ _
6 r _ _
7 j _ _ _
8 f _ _
9 c _ _ _
10 s _ _ _ _ _ _ _ _ _

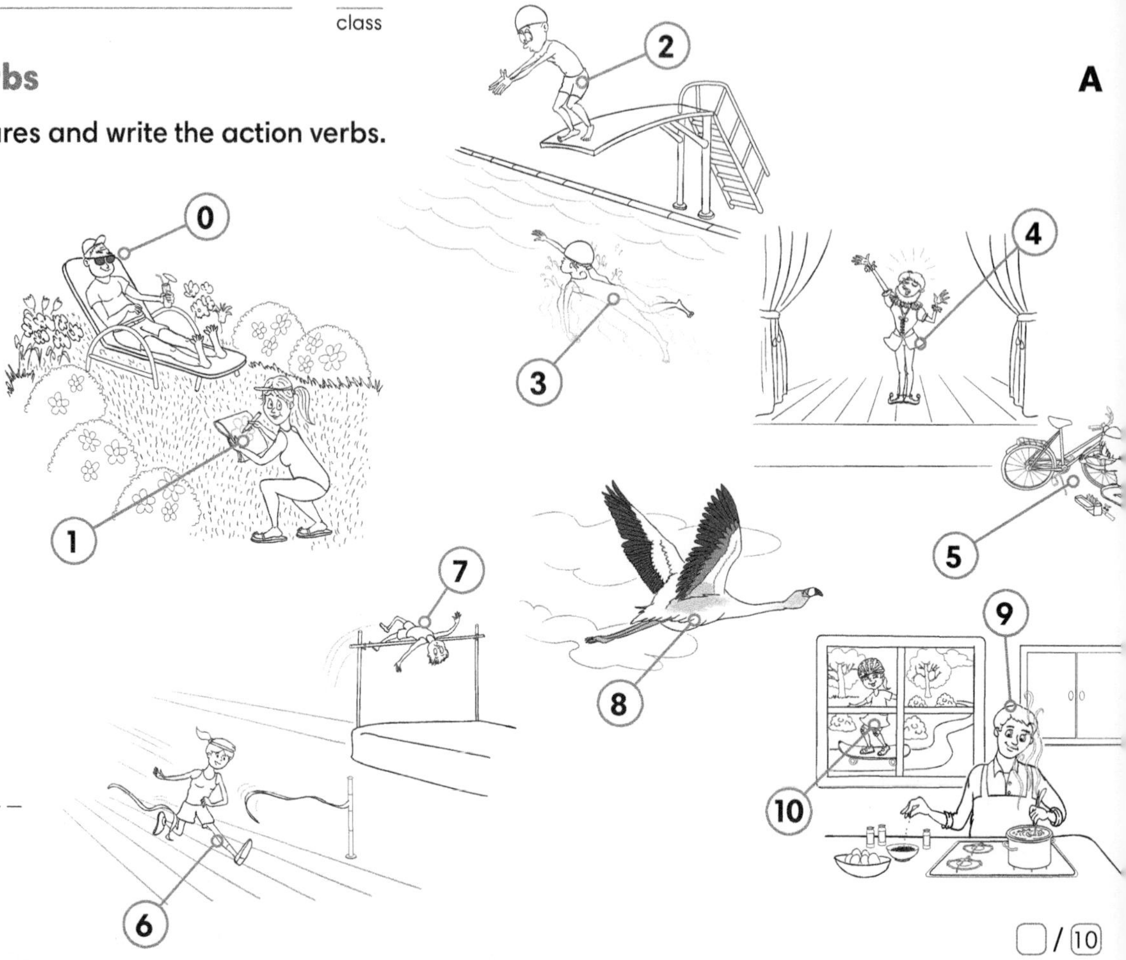

/10

2 Complete the phrases with the words in the box. There is one extra word.

climb cook read ride sing ~~work~~ write

0 *work* in pairs
1 ________ a book
2 ________ your name
3 ________ a tree
4 ________ a bike
5 ________ a song

/5

name ______________________ class ______

5.2 *Make, play, ride*

A

3 Match sentences 1–5 with words a–e.

My family is very talented.

0 Dad can play [*f*]
1 Mum can make [ ]
2 I can ride [ ]
3 My big sister can play the [ ]
4 My brother can make a [ ]
5 My baby sister can play [ ]

a guitar.
b cupcakes.
c a horse.
d fantastic poster.
e computer games.
f football.

What about you? What can you do?

/5

Your total score /20

name _____ class _____

B

5.1 Action verbs

1 Look at the pictures and write the action verbs.

0 s _i t_

1 d _ _ _

2 f _ _

3 r _ _

4 j _ _ _

5 c _ _ _

6 s _ _ _ _ _ _ _ _

7 a _ _

8 f _ _

9 d _ _ _

10 s _ _ _

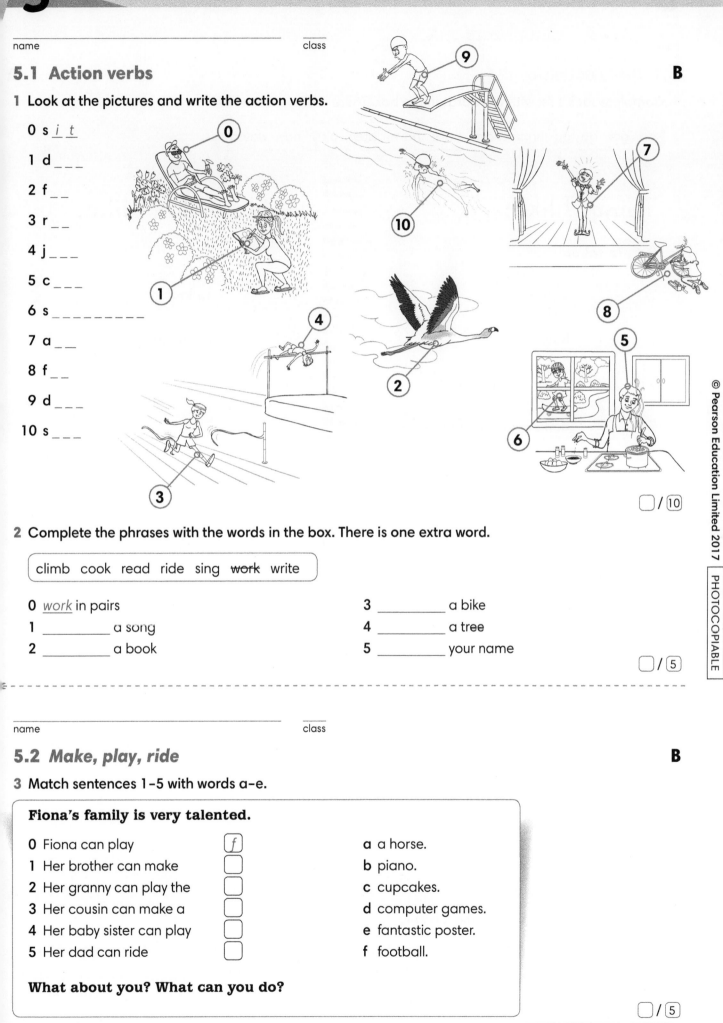

☐ / ⑩

2 Complete the phrases with the words in the box. There is one extra word.

climb cook read ride sing ~~work~~ write

0 _work_ in pairs

1 _____ a song

2 _____ a book

3 _____ a bike

4 _____ a tree

5 _____ your name

☐ / ⑤

- -

name _____ class _____

5.2 *Make, play, ride*

B

3 Match sentences 1–5 with words a–e.

Fiona's family is very talented.

0 Fiona can play   ☐ _f_   a a horse.

1 Her brother can make   ☐   b piano.

2 Her granny can play the ☐   c cupcakes.

3 Her cousin can make a   ☐   d computer games.

4 Her baby sister can play ☐   e fantastic poster.

5 Her dad can ride   ☐   f football.

What about you? What can you do?

☐ / ⑤

Your total score ☐ / ⑳

19

6 Vocabulary Check A

name ______________________ class ______

6.1 Daily activities **A**

1 Complete Jack's list with the words in the box. There is one extra word.

do get ~~go~~ go hang have have have listen play tidy watch

Things I like:

0 *go* to school

1 ________ a shower

2 ________ lessons

3 ________ out with my friends

4 ________ dinner with my family

5 ________ TV

6 ________ to music

Things I don't like:

7 ________ up

8 ________ to bed

9 ________ my room

10 ________ my homework

☐ / 10

name ______________________ class ______

6.3 Days of the week **A**

2 Complete the sentences with the days of the week.

0 On T *u e s d a y* s I see my friends at school.

1 On F _ _ _ _ s my sister swims in the sea.

2 On W _ _ _ _ _ _ _ s we go to Aunt Magda's house.

3 On Th _ _ _ _ _ s I finish school early.

4 On Sa _ _ _ _ _ s my mum, my dad, my sister and I work in the garden.

5 On M _ _ _ _ s you and I play football at school.

☐ / 5

name ______________________ class ______

6.4 Months **A**

3 Complete the sentences with the months.

0 Hi, I'm Mike. My birthday is in *March*. (month 3)

1 My friend's birthday is in ________. (month 8)

2 My mum's birthday is in ________. (month 2)

3 My dad's birthday is in ________. (month 4)

4 My cousin's birthday is in ________. (month 10)

5 My sister's birthday is in ________. (month 6)

☐ / 5

Your total score ☐ / 20

6 Vocabulary Check B

name ______________________ class ______

6.1 Daily activities B

1 Complete Jack's list with the words in the box. There is one extra word.

do get ~~go~~ go hang have have have listen play tidy watch

Things I like:

0 *go* to school
1 ________ to music
2 ________ a shower
3 ________ TV
4 ________ out with my friends
5 ________ lessons
6 ________ lunch with my grandparents

Things I don't like:

7 ________ my homework
8 ________ up
9 ________ my room
10 ________ to bed

/ 10

name ______________________ class ______

6.3 Days of the week B

2 Complete the sentences with the days of the week.

0 On **T** *u e s d a y* **s** I help my friend with her homework.
1 On **M** _ _ _ _ _ **s** my dad comes home late.
2 On **Th** _ _ _ _ _ _ **s** you and I play football at school.
3 On **W** _ _ _ _ _ _ _ _ **s** we finish school early.
4 On **Sa** _ _ _ _ _ _ **s** my mum works in the garden.
5 On **S** _ _ _ _ _ **s** we go to Uncle Jim's house.

/ 5

name ______________________ class ______

6.4 Months B

3 Complete the sentences with the months.

0 Hi, I'm Luke. My birthday is in *March*. (month 3)
1 My brother's birthday is in ________. (month 1)
2 My sister's birthday is in ________. (month 7)
3 My granny's birthday is in ________. (month 5)
4 My best friend's birthday is in ________. (month 9)
5 My cousin's birthday is in ________. (month 12)

/ 5

Your total score / 20

name _____ class _____

7.1 Wild animals

A

1 Look at the pictures and complete the sentences.

0 A t <u>i g e r</u> is a big cat.

1 A m _ _ _ _ y can climb trees.

2 A s _ _ _ e hasn't got any legs.

3 A k _ _ g _ _ _ o can jump.

4 A b _ t _ _ _ _ _ y can fly.

5 A s _ _ _ _ r has got eight legs.

6 A f _ _ g can swim and jump.

7 A f _ _ _ can swim but it can't walk.

8 A w _ _ _ e can swim. It's very, very big!

9 A g _ _ _ f _ e has got a long neck.

10 A cr _ _ _ _ _ _ _ can swim. It's got big teeth!

☐ / ⑩

- -

name _____ class _____

7.2 Pets

A

2 Match words 1–5 with sentences a–f. There is one extra sentence.

0 dog ☐ *g*

1 iguana ☐

2 tortoise ☐

3 parrot ☐

4 goldfish ☐

5 hamster ☐

a It's got four legs but it can't run and it can't climb trees.

b It's orange. It can swim but it can't walk.

c It can fly and it can talk.

d It's green and it can climb trees.

e It's a very small animal. It's usually brown.

f It's got long ears. It isn't very clever.

g It can run and jump but it can't climb trees.

☐ / ⑤

- -

name _____ class _____

7.5 Adjectives

A

3 Complete the sentences with adjectives.

0 Lions are f <u>a s</u> t.

1 Baby animals are c _ _ e.

2 Crocodiles are d _ _ _ _ _ _ _ s.

3 Tortoises are s _ _ w.

4 Elephants are s _ _ _ _ g.

5 Spiders are u _ _ y.

☐ / ⑤

Your total score ☐ / ⑳

22

7 Vocabulary Check B

name ______________________ class ______

7.1 Wild animals **B**

1 Look at the pictures and complete the sentences.

0 A t *i g e r* is a big cat.
1 A **s** _ _ _ **e** hasn't got legs.
2 A **l** _ _ _ is a big cat too.
3 A **gi** _ _ _ _ **e** has got a long neck.
4 An **e** _ _ _ _ _ _ **t** has got a long nose.
5 A **c** _ _ _ _ _ _ **le** has got big teeth.
6 A **b** _ _ _ can fly.
7 A **s** _ _ _ _ **r** has got eight legs.
8 A **f** _ _ _ can swim and jump.
9 A **w** _ _ _ **e** can swim but it isn't a fish.
10 A **k** _ _ **g** _ _ _ _ can jump.

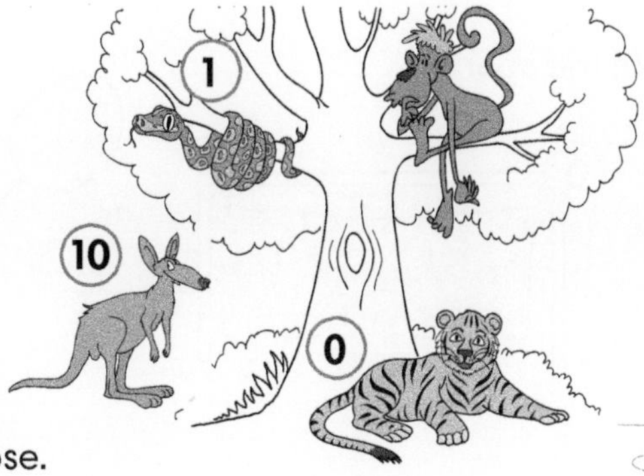

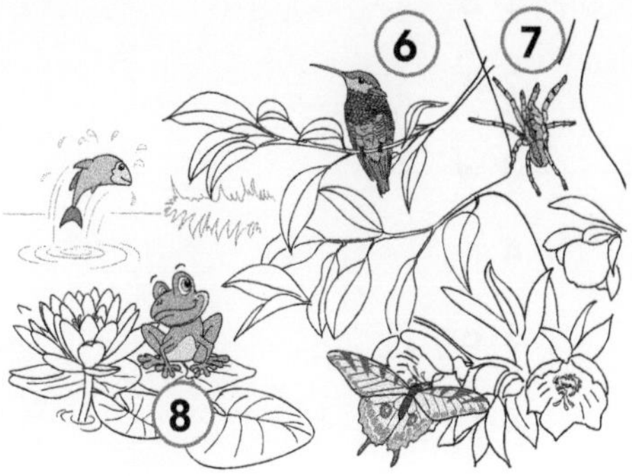

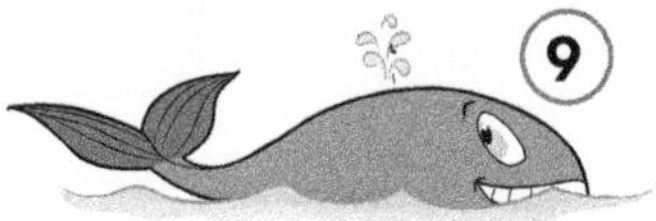

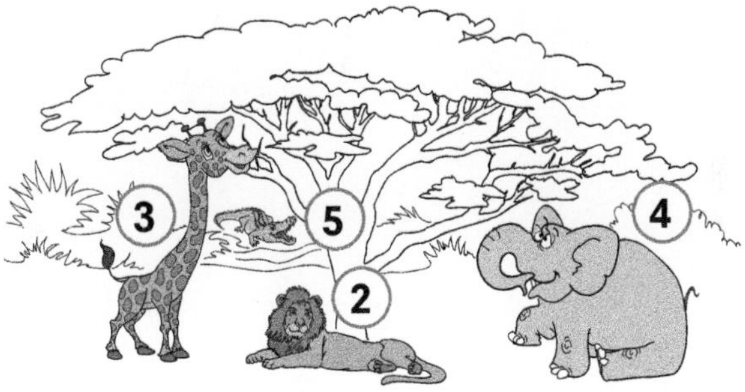

☐ / 10

name ______________________ class ______

7.2 Pets **B**

2 Match words 1-5 with sentences a-f. There is one extra sentence.

0 dog [*g*]
1 goldfish [ ]
2 iguana [ ]
3 hamster [ ]
4 tortoise [ ]
5 parrot [ ]

a It's green and it can climb trees.
b It's got four legs but it can't run and it can't climb trees.
c It's a very small animal. It's usually brown.
d It's orange. It can swim but it can't walk.
e It's got long ears. It isn't very clever.
f It can fly and it can talk.
g It can run and jump but it can't climb trees.

☐ / 5

name ______________________ class ______

7.5 Adjectives **B**

3 Complete the sentences with adjectives.

0 Lions are **f** *a s* **t**.
1 Elephants are **s** _ _ _ _ **g**.
2 Baby animals are **c** _ _ **e**.
3 Spiders are **u** _ _ **y**.
4 Tortoises are **s** _ _ **w**.
5 Crocodiles are **d** _ _ _ _ _ _ _ **s**.

☐ / 5

Your total score ☐ / 20

8 Vocabulary Check A

name ______________________ class ______

8.1 Sports

A

1 Look at the pictures and write the sports.

0 f*ootball*

1 b _ _ _ _ _ _ _ _

2 h _ _ _ _ _

3 w _ _ _ _ _ _ _ _ _ _

4 r _ _ _ _ _ s _ _ _ _ _ _

5 c _ _ _ _ _ _

6 t _ _ _ _ t _ _ _ _ _

7 i _ _-s _ _ _ _ _ _

8 b _ _ _ _ _ _ _ _ _

9 s _ _ _ _ _ _

10 s _ _ _ _ _

0 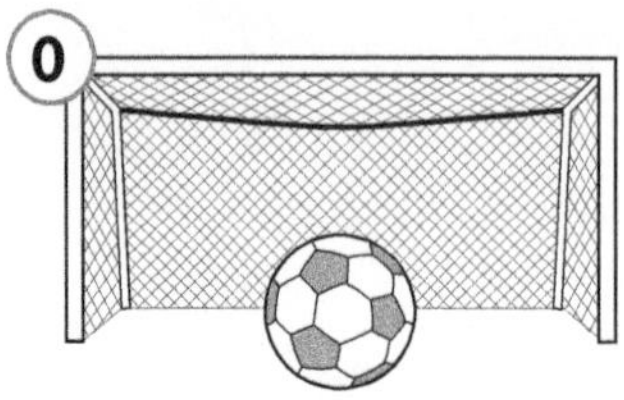
1 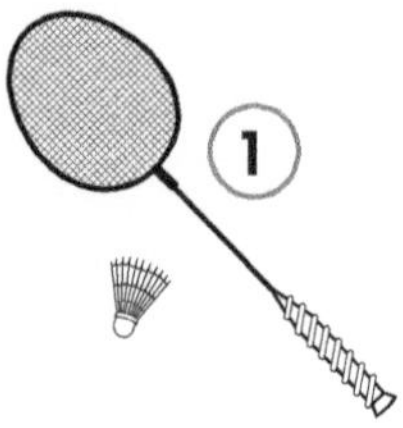
2 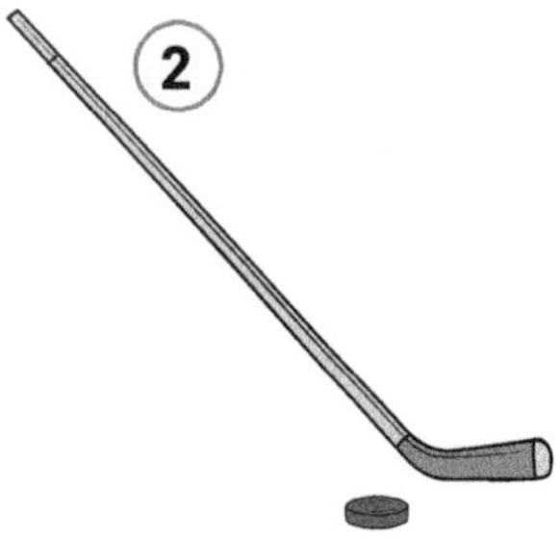
3 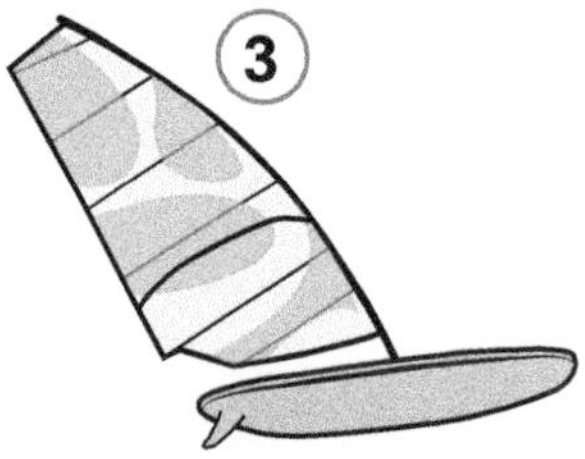
4 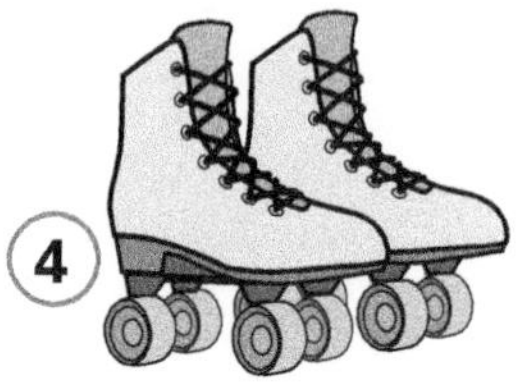
5 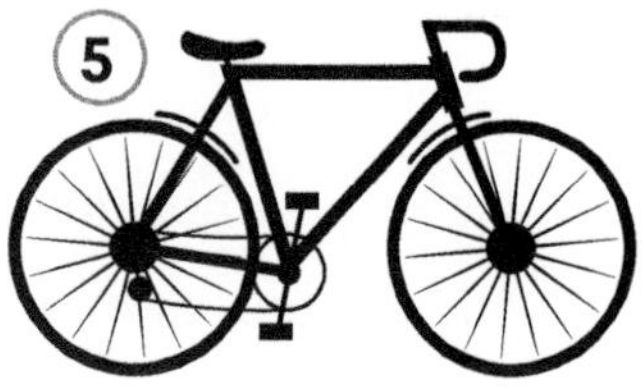
6 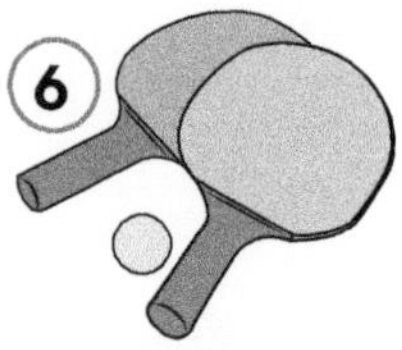
7 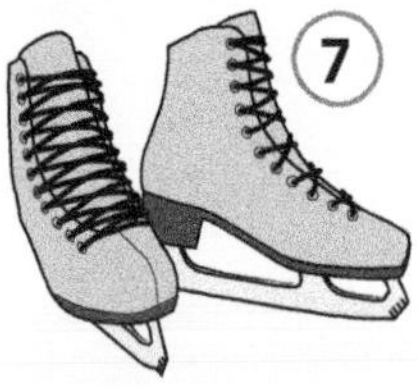
8 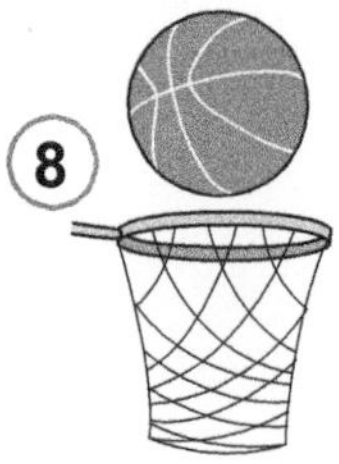
9 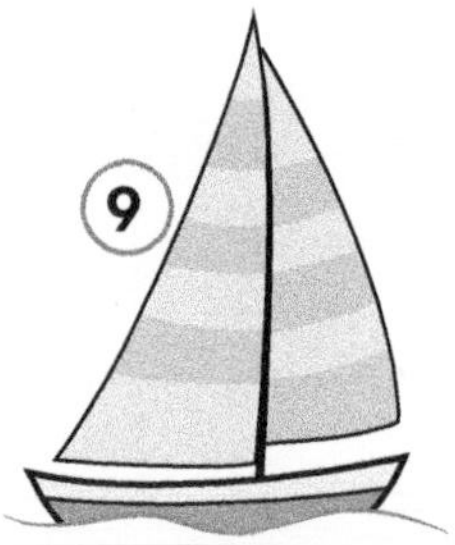
10 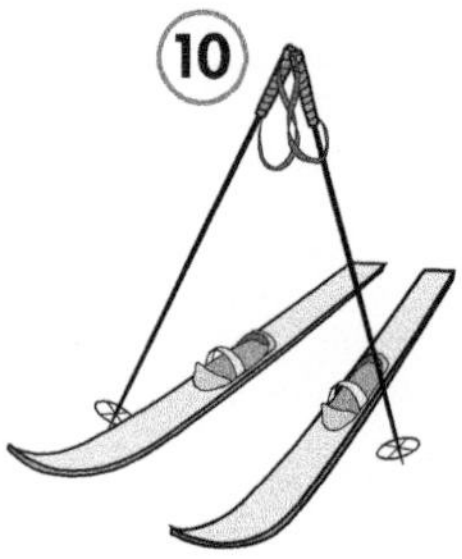

☐ / 10

2 Complete the sentences with *do*, *go* or *play*.

0 I often *go* swimming.
1 I ________ taekwondo on Tuesdays and Fridays.
2 I ________ hockey at school.
3 I ________ windsurfing with my friends.
4 I never ________ roller skating.
5 I ________ basketball on Saturdays.

☐ / 5

---

name ______________________ class ______

8.5 Healthy lifestyle

A

3 Complete the text with the words in the box. There is one extra word.

brush do drink eat ~~go~~ have play

Do you want to be heathy?

0 *Go* to bed early.
1 ____________ your teeth after every meal.
2 ____________ a lot of water.
3 ____________ fruit and vegetables.
4 ____________ exercise every day.
5 ____________ friends.

☐ / 5

Your total score ☐ / 20

name _____   class _____

8.1 Sports

B

1 Look at the pictures and write the sports.

0 f <u>o o t b a l l</u>

1 b _ _ _ _ _ _ _ _ _

2 i _ _ -s _ _ _ _ _ _

3 h _ _ _ _ _

4 b _ _ _ _ _ _ _ _

5 s _ _ _ _ _ _

6 w _ _ _ _ _ _ _ _ _ _

7 s _ _ _ _ _

8 t _ _ _ _ t _ _ _ _ _

9 r _ _ _ _ _ s _ _ _ _ _ _

10 c _ _ _ _ _ _

☐ / ⑩

2 Complete the sentences with _do_, _go_ or _play_.

0 I often <u>go</u> swimming.

1 On Saturdays I _____ skateboarding.

2 On Mondays and Wednesdays I _____ hockey.

3 I don't _____ taekwondo. I don't like it.

4 I _____ volleyball at school.

5 I _____ skiing in the winter.

☐ / ⑤

- -

name _____   class _____

8.5 Healthy lifestyle

B

3 Complete the text with the words in the box. There is one extra word.

| brush   do   drink   eat   ~~go~~   have   play |

Do you want to be heathy?

0 <u>Go</u> to bed early.

1 _____ exercise every day.

2 _____ fruit and vegetables.

3 _____ a lot of water.

4 _____ your teeth after every meal.

5 _____ friends.

☐ / ⑤

Your total score ☐ / ⑳   **25**

Grammar Check A

name _____ class _____

1.2 *To be affirmative*   A

1 Circle the correct word.

0 Kit *am* /*is* / *are* Superdug's best friend.
1 You *am* / *is* / *are* eleven years old.
2 I *am* / *is* / *are* Fred and Sue's daughter.
3 My classmates *am* / *is* / *are* at school.
4 His neighbour *am* / *is* / *are* in the garden.
5 You and your family *am* / *is* / *are* Italian.

◯ / ⑤

1.2 Possessives

2 Complete the sentences. Use the words in the box.

| her   his   Magda's   my   ~~your~~   your |

0 You're at school, but <u>your</u> parents are at home.
1 The girl is happy. It's _____ birthday today.
2 James is on holiday with _____ parents.
3 Tim's bag is green and _____ bag is green too.
4 I'm Anna. This is _____ friend, Charlie.
5 Happy birthday, Alice. Here's _____ present.

◯ / ⑤

name _____ class _____

1.3 *To be negative*   A

3 Write negative sentences. Use 'm not, isn't, aren't.

0 Robin <u>isn't</u> in the park today.
1 My friends and I _____ superheroes.
2 You _____ Italian. Your family is from Spain.
3 I _____ Daniella's cousin.
4 My parents _____ French. Dad is from Poland and Mum is from Spain.
5 My aunt _____ Polish. Her parents are from the UK.

◯ / ⑤

Your total score ◯ / ⑮

26

Grammar Check B

name _____ class _____

1.2 *To be affirmative*   B

1 Circle the correct word.

0 Kit *am* /*is* / *are* Superdug's best friend.
1 My parents *am* / *is* / *are* at home.
2 You *am* / *is* / *are* Alan and Gina's son.
3 Her cousin *am* / *is* / *are* on holiday.
4 I *am* / *is* / *are* very happy today.
5 The birthday card *am* / *is* / *are* from your friend.

◯ / ⑤

1.2 Possessives

2 Complete the sentences. Use the words in the box.

| her   his   Julie's   my   ~~your~~   your |

0 You're at school, but <u>your</u> parents are at home.
1 I'm at school, but _____ parents are at home.
2 Mary is British. _____ family is from London.
3 Happy birthday, Johnnie. Here's _____ birthday cake.
4 The boy is in the park with _____ friends.
5 Sam's bag is black but _____ bag is blue.

◯ / ⑤

name _____ class _____

1.3 *To be negative*   B

3 Write negative sentences. Use 'm not, isn't, aren't.

0 Robin <u>isn't</u> in the park today.
1 My aunt and uncle _____ British. My aunt is from the USA and my uncle is from Spain.
2 His classmates and teachers _____ on holiday.
3 Emily's uncle _____ French. His parents are from Poland.
4 You _____ twelve years old! It isn't your birthday today.
5 I _____ at my granny's house.

◯ / ⑤

Your total score ◯ / ⑮

2 Grammar Check A

name ______________________ class ________

2.2 *This / that / these / those* A

1 Complete the sentences with *this*, *that*, *these* or *those*.

0 *This* is Jim's cap. ⇒

1 __________ boots are cool. ⇒

2 __________ are new trousers. ⇒

3 __________ coat is long. ⇒

4 __________ jacket is too big. ⇒

5 __________ are Maria's trainers. ⇒

☐ / 5

name ______________________ class ________

2.3 *To be* questions A

2 Make questions.

0 we / cool / are / ?
Are we cool?

1 they / are / in the park / ?
____

2 your / is / colour / what / favourite / ?
____

3 boring / I / am / ?
____

4 are / a superhero / you / ?
____

5 Anna's / she / is / best friend / ?
____

☐ / 5

2.3 *To be* short answers

3 Complete the short answers.

0 **A:** Is the boy in the garden?
B: No, *he isn't*.

1 **A:** Are you Dug's mum?
B: Yes, ______________________ .

2 **A:** Are Diana and I good students?
B: Yes, ______________________ .

3 **A:** Is David's hoodie cool?
B: No, ______________________ .

4 **A:** Are you and Peter at home?
B: No, ______________________ .

5 **A:** Are Jane and Fred best friends?
B: Yes, ______________________ .

☐ / 5

Your total score ☐ / 15

2 Grammar Check B

name ______________________ class ________

2.2 *This / that / these / those* B

1 Complete the sentences with *this*, *that*, *these* or *those*.

0 *That* is Anna's T-shirt. ⇒

1 __________ shoes are new. ⇒

2 __________ are Lucy's jeans. ⇒

3 __________ hoodie is too small. ⇒

4 __________ cap is too big. ⇒

5 __________ are cool shoes. ⇒

☐ / 5

name ______________________ class ________

2.3 *To be* questions B

2 Make questions.

0 we / cool / are / ?
Are we cool?

1 I / am / best friend / your / ?
____

2 Superdug's / are / brother / you / ?
____

3 long / they / are / trousers / ?
____

4 a superhero / he / is / ?
____

5 is / what / film / favourite / your / ?
____

☐ / 5

2.3 *To be* short answers

3 Complete the short answers.

0 **A:** Is the boy in the garden?
B: No, *he isn't*.

1 **A:** Are Nick and Sam best friends?
B: Yes, ______________________ .

2 **A:** Are you happy at school?
B: No, ______________________ .

3 **A:** Are you and your parents on holiday?
B: Yes, ______________________ .

4 **A:** Are Suzie and I good students?
B: Yes, ______________________ .

5 **A:** Is Flora's tracksuit new?
B: No, ______________________ .

☐ / 5

Your total score ☐ / 15

3 Grammar Check A

name ______________________ class ________

3.2 *There is / there are* affirmative A

1 Circle the correct answer.

0 (*There's*) / *There are* a tree in the garden.
1 *There's / There are* three desks in the classroom.
2 *There's / There are* one bathroom in the house.
3 *There's / There are* five posters on the wall.
4 *There's / There are* two rats under the sofa.
5 *There's / There are* a bed in the bedroom.

☐ / 5

name ______________________ class ________

3.3 *There is / there are* negative A

2 Make negative sentences.

0 there / in / isn't / a desk / the kitchen
There isn't a desk in the kitchen.
1 aren't/two/armchairs/the bedroom/in/there
____
2 apple trees/the garden/four/there/in/aren't
____
3 on / there / a bag / isn't / the floor
____
4 there / a computer / isn't / the table / on
____

☐ / 4

3.3 *There is / there are* questions and short answers

3 Complete the dialogues with the words in the box.

are are ~~is~~ ~~is~~ is no there yes

A: [0]*Is* there a book on the desk?
B: Yes, there [0]*is*, but there isn't a pencil.

A: [1]__________ there two DVDs on the table?
B: Yes, there [2]__________.

A: Is [3]__________ a chair in the living room?
B: [4]__________, there isn't.

A: [5]__________ there a T-shirt in the wardrobe?
B: [6]__________, there is and there's a tracksuit too.

☐ / 6

Your total score ☐ / 15

3 Grammar Check B

name ______________________ class ________

3.2 *There is / there are* affirmative B

1 Circle the correct answer.

0 (*There's*) / *There are* a tree in the garden.
1 *There's / There are* twenty DVDs in the room.
2 *There's / There are* sixteen students in the room.
3 *There's / There are* a fridge in the kitchen.
4 *There's / There are* one bed in the bedroom.
5 *There's / There are* two shoes under the bed.

☐ / 5

name ______________________ class ________

3.3 *There is / there are* negative B

2 Make negative sentences.

0 there / in / isn't / a desk / the kitchen
There isn't a desk in the kitchen.
1 girls / your family / four / there / in / aren't
____
2 aren't / two / the garage / cars / in / there
____
3 on / there / a poster / isn't / the wall
____
4 there / a phone / isn't / on the table
____

☐ / 4

3.3 *There is / there are* questions and short answers

3 Complete the dialogues with the words in the box.

are aren't ~~is~~ ~~is~~ is no there yes

A: [0]*Is* there a book on the desk?
B: Yes, there [0]*is*, but there isn't a pencil.

A: [1]__________ there two DVDs in your bedroom?
B: No, there [2]__________, but there are two DVDs in the living room.

A: Is [3]__________ a table in the kitchen?
B: [4]__________, there isn't.

A: [5]__________ there a rat in the garage?
B: [6]__________, there is but there isn't a rat in the house!

☐ / 6

Your total score ☐ / 15

4 Grammar Check A

name ______________________ class ______

4.2 *Have got* affirmative and negative **A**

1 Circle the correct word.

0 You *have got* / *has got* white teeth.
1 He *have got* / *has got* ten fingers.
2 We *haven't got* / *hasn't got* long legs.
3 She *haven't got* / *hasn't got* blue hair.
4 I *haven't got* / *hasn't got* wavy hair.
5 They *have got* / *has got* big feet.

☐ / 5

name ______________________ class ______

4.3 *Have got* questions and short answers **A**

2 Complete the dialogues with the words in the box.

got has hasn't ~~have~~ have have haven't ~~yes~~

A: [0]*Have* you got wavy hair? **B:** [0]*Yes*, I have.

A: [1]__________ Maria got long blond hair?
B: No, she [2]__________.

A: Have you and Alex [3]__________ blue eyes?
B: Yes, we [4]__________.

A: [5]__________ Jane and I got white teeth?
B: No, you [6]__________.

☐ / 6

4.3 *Its, our, your, their*

3 Complete the sentences with the words in the box. There is one extra word.

its ~~our~~ our their their your

0 **We**'ve got wavy hair.
Our hair is wavy.
1 **The dog** has got short legs.
__________ legs are short.
2 **The students** have got good marks.
__________ marks are good.
3 **Jack and I** have got brown hair.
__________ hair is brown.
4 **You and Anna** have got a nice brother.
__________ brother is nice.

☐ / 4

Your total score ☐ / 15

4 Grammar Check B

name ______________________ class ______

4.2 *Have got* affirmative and negative **B**

1 Circle the correct word.

0 You *have got* / *has got* white teeth.
1 She *have got* / *has got* ten toes.
2 I *haven't got* / *hasn't got* superpowers.
3 We *haven't got* / *hasn't got* curly red hair.
4 He *haven't got* / *hasn't got* blond hair.
5 They *have got* / *has got* small ears.

☐ / 5

name ______________________ class ______

4.3 *Have got* questions and short answers **B**

2 Complete the dialogues with the words in the box.

got has hasn't ~~have~~ have have no ~~yes~~

A: [0]*Have* you got wavy hair? **B:** [0]*Yes*, I have.

A: Have my sister and I [1]__________ white teeth?
B: [2]__________, you haven't.

A: [3]__________ your grandad got a small house?
B: No, he [4]__________

A: [5]__________ you and Bob got long legs?
B: Yes, we [6]__________.

☐ / 6

4.3 *Its, our, your, their*

3 Complete the sentences with the words in the box. There is one extra word.

its ~~our~~ our their their your

0 **We**'ve got wavy hair.
Our hair is wavy.
1 **The dogs** have got long ears.
__________ ears are long.
2 **The house** has got big rooms.
__________ rooms are big.
3 **You and your dad** have got brown eyes.
__________ eyes are brown.
4 **My classmates and I** have got a helpful teacher.
__________ teacher is helpful.

☐ / 4

Your total score ☐ / 15

© Pearson Education Limited 2017 PHOTOCOPIABLE

5 Grammar Check A

name ____________________ class ______

5.2 *Can* affirmative and negative A

1 Write sentences with *can* [✓] or *can't* [✗].

0 you / ride a bike ✗ *You can't ride a bike.*
1 my mother / make great cupcakes ✓
____
2 I / fix the television ✓
____
3 Clara and her best friend / speak English ✗
____
4 Superdug / do clever things with computers ✗
____
5 my brother and I / play the piano ✓
____

[ ] / [5]

name ____________________ class ______

5.3 *Can* questions A

2 Make questions.

0 you / ten / make / can / posters / ?
Can you make ten posters?
1 Jack and I / home / go / can / ?
____
2 this / can / your dad / camera / fix / ?
____
3 mum / can / what / do / your / ?
____
4 words / the students / can / read / difficult / ?
____
5 Betty's / fast / can / run / dog / ?
____

[ ] / [5]

5.3 *Can* short answers

3 Give positive [☺] or negative [☹] answers.

0 A: Can you cook well? ☺ B: *Yes, I can.*
1 A: Can your parents sing? ☹ B: __________
2 A: Can your dad fix things? ☺ B: __________
3 A: Can the dog fly? ☹ B: __________
4 A: Can we go to the park? ☺ B: __________
5 A: Can you and Ben swim? ☹ B: __________

[ ] / [5]

Your total score [ ] / [15]

5 Grammar Check B

name ____________________ class ______

5.2 *Can* affirmative and negative B

1 Write sentences with *can* [✓] or *can't* [✗].

0 you / ride a bike ✗ *You can't ride a bike.*
1 Max and his best friend / speak English ✗
____
2 my sister and I / play the guitar ✓
____
3 his aunt / make cakes ✗
____
4 Kit's friend / do clever things with computers ✓
____
5 I / fix the radio ✗
____

[ ] / [5]

name ____________________ class ______

5.3 *Can* questions B

2 Make questions.

0 you / ten / make / can / posters / ?
Can you make ten posters?
1 stories / the students / can / good / write / ?
____
2 computer / that / can / fix / your brother / ?
____
3 Molly and I / home / go / can / ?
____
4 fast / Ryan's / can / run / horse / ?
____
5 best friend / can / what / do / your / ?
____

[ ] / [5]

5.3 *Can* short answers

3 Give positive [☺] or negative [☹] answers.

0 A: Can you cook well? ☺ B: *Yes, I can.*
1 A: Can zebras run fast? ☺ B: __________
2 A: Can you and Jill act? ☹ B: __________
3 A: Can his mum cook well? ☺ B: __________
4 A: Can Roger play the piano? ☹ B: __________
5 A: Can Tim and I go home? ☺ B: __________

[ ] / [5]

Your total score [ ] / [15]

6 Grammar Check A

name _______________ class ____

6.2 Present Simple affirmative A

1 Circle the correct word.

0 I (get) / gets up early.
1 We *hang* / *hangs* out with our friends.
2 Barry *listen* / *listens* to music in his room.
3 Mum *cook* / *cooks* great food!
4 The girls *draw* / *draws* well.
5 You *run* / *runs* very fast!

☐ / [5]

2 Complete the sentences with the Present Simple form of the verbs.

0 Julie *watches* TV. (watch)
1 Mum _______________ a shower. (have)
2 Dad _______________ dinner. (make)
3 Dave _______________ things. (fix)
4 Diana _______________ her homework. (do)
5 Greg _______________ his room. (tidy)

☐ / [5]

name _______________ class ____

6.3 Adverbs of frequency A

3 Make sentences.

0 I / English / have / never / lessons / on Monday
I never have English lessons on Monday.
1 always / my classmates and I / our / do / homework
____
2 listens / often / music / to / Nesta
____
3 football / sometimes / the boys / play
____
4 early / usually / to / grandad / my / goes / bed
____
5 Thursday / are / Ania / never / Ewa / late / and / on
____

☐ / [5]

Your total score ☐ / [15]

6 Grammar Check B

name _______________ class ____

6.2 Present Simple affirmative B

1 Circle the correct word.

0 I (get) / gets up early.
1 The boys *climb* / *climbs* walls.
2 Edith *listen* / *listens* to music in her room.
3 We *hang* / *hangs* out with our friends.
4 Dad *play* / *plays* the guitar.
5 You *draw* / *draws* well.

☐ / [5]

2 Complete the sentences with the Present Simple form of the verbs.

0 Julie *watches* TV. (watch)
1 Harry _______________ bikes and cars. (fix)
2 Cassie _______________ the living room. (tidy)
3 Mandy _______________ her homework. (do)
4 Granny _______________ great cakes. (make)
5 Dad _______________ a shower. (have)

☐ / [5]

name _______________ class ____

6.3 Adverbs of frequency B

3 Make sentences.

0 I / English / have / never / lessons / on Monday
I never have English lessons on Monday.
1 sometimes / the girls / tennis / play
____
2 our / my friends and I / homework / do / always
____
3 parents / usually / to / early / my / go / work
____
4 and / Julia / never / on / late / Tuesday / her sisters / are
____
5 listens / to / often / Gerry / music
____

☐ / [5]

Your total score ☐ / [15]

© Pearson Education Limited 2017 PHOTOCOPIABLE

name   class

7.2 Present Simple negative   **A**

1 Complete the sentences with the negative form of the verbs.

0 I **want** a dog but my parents *don't want* a dog.

1 You **feed** your dog at seven o'clock but your neighbour _____ his dog at seven.

2 My mum **likes** computer games but my grandparents _____ computer games.

3 The lion **has** big teeth but the tortoise _____ big teeth.

4 My sister and I **walk** to school but you _____ to school. You ride your bike.

5 Fred and Harriet **take** their dog to the park but Sharon _____ her dog to the park.

☐ / ⑤

name   class

7.3 Present Simple questions and short answers   **A**

2 Add *do* or *does* to make questions.

0 *Do* you like animals?

1 _____ these animals live in Africa?

2 _____ Superdug have dinner with Kit?

3 _____ your sister tidy her bedroom on Saturdays?

4 _____ Alex and Jane watch TV in the evening?

5 _____ his mother get up early?

☐ / ⑤

3 Complete the dialogue with short answers.

Jim: Do you get up early?

Beth: **0***Yes, I do*. I always get up early.

Jim: Does your mum cook breakfast for the family?

Beth: **1**_____. Dad cooks breakfast.

Jim: Do your sisters ride their bikes to school?

Beth: **2**_____. They walk to school.

Jim: Does your friend Luke go to your school?

Beth: **3**_____. We go together.

Jim: Do you and Luke do your homework?

Beth: **4**_____. We always do it after school.

Jim: Does your swimming lesson start at five?

Beth: **5**_____. It starts at four.

☐ / ⑤

Your total score ☐ / ⑮

32

name   class

7.2 Present Simple negative   **B**

1 Complete the sentences with the negative form of the verbs.

0 I **want** a dog but my parents *don't want* a dog.

1 Mandy and Carl **do** their homework in the afternoon but my brother and I _____ our homework in the afternoon.

2 The lion **runs** fast but the tortoise _____ fast.

3 I **cook** lunch at one o'clock but Joe _____ lunch at one o'clock. He cooks it at two.

4 My cousin Beth **likes** music but I _____ music.

5 You **get** up early on Saturdays but your sister _____ up early on Saturdays.

☐ / ⑤

name   class

7.3 Present Simple questions and short answers   **B**

2 Add *do* or *does* to make questions.

0 *Do* you like animals?

1 _____ your dad tidy his room on Mondays?

2 _____ her brother go to bed late?

3 _____ Kit have lunch with Superdug?

4 _____ those animals live in India?

5 _____ Suzie and Pete often listen to music?

☐ / ⑤

3 Complete the dialogue with short answers.

Polly: Do you get up early?

Rob: **0***Yes, I do*. I always get up early.

Polly: Does your dad have a shower in the morning?

Rob: **1**_____. He always has a shower before breakfast.

Polly: Do your brothers walk to school?

Rob: **2**_____. They ride their bikes.

Polly: Does your friend Tom go to your school?

Rob: **3**_____. We go to school together.

Polly: Does your piano lesson start at four o'clock?

Rob: **4**_____. It starts at three o'clock.

Polly: Do you and Tom do your homework?

Rob: **5**_____. We always do it in the evening.

☐ / ⑤

Your total score ☐ / ⑮

8 Grammar Check A

name _____ class _____

8.2 *Love/like/don't like/hate + -ing* **A**

1 Complete the sentences with the correct form of the verb.

0 My parents love _playing_ (play) tennis.
1 I don't like _____ (swim).
2 Sally likes _____ (sing).
3 Do you hate _____ (do) sports?
4 Zoe and I love _____ (run).
5 Jan likes _____ (write) stories.

☐ / ⑤

8.2 Object pronouns

2 Complete the sentences with the words in the box. There is one extra word.

> her him it me them us ~~you~~

0 You're my sister and I love _you_.
1 I like this music. Let's listen to _____!
2 She can act well. I want to watch _____.
3 Are you my friend? Do you like _____?
4 We've got great teachers and we listen to _____.
5 We like you. Please hang out with _____.

☐ / ⑤

---

name _____ class _____

8.3 Question words   **A**

3 Match questions 1–5 and answers a–f. There is one extra answer.

0 What are those animals? ☐ g
1 Who is that girl? ☐
2 When do you go to school? ☐
3 How many boats can you see? ☐
4 Whose jumper is this? ☐
5 Where do they live? ☐

a In Warsaw.
b My cousin Julia.
c Fifteen.
d At eight o'clock.
e It's Maria's.
f These are my clothes.
g They're monkeys.

☐ / ⑤

Your total score ☐ / ⑮

8 Grammar Check B

name _____ class _____

8.2 *Love/like/don't like/hate + -ing* **B**

1 Complete the sentences with the correct form of the verb.

0 My parents love _playing_ (play) tennis.
1 Kate likes _____ (cook).
2 Does he like _____ (read) books?
3 You don't like _____ (ride) horses.
4 Linda and I hate _____ (run).
5 I love _____ (swim).

☐ / ⑤

8.2 Object pronouns

2 Complete the sentences with the words in the box. There is one extra word.

> her him it me them us ~~you~~

0 You're my sister and I love _you_.
1 They are my parents and they love _____.
2 Ice-skating is fun. Let's watch _____.
3 My brother is at the party. Can you see _____?
4 We like you. Please hang out with _____.
5 Aunt Mary and Uncle Joe are great. We love _____.

☐ / ⑤

---

name _____ class _____

8.3 Question words   **B**

3 Match questions 1–5 and answers a–f. There is one extra answer.

0 What are those animals? ☐ g
1 How many birds can you see? ☐
2 Who are those people? ☐
3 Whose jeans are they? ☐
4 Where does he play football? ☐
5 When do you go to bed? ☐

a My mum and dad.
b At school.
c At half past ten.
d It's a zebra.
e They're Lee's.
f Eleven.
g They're monkeys.

☐ / ⑤

Your total score ☐ / ⑮

33

name _______________ class _____

Vocabulary

1 Write the numbers.

0 8 *eight*
1 11 ____________
2 14 ____________
3 43 ____________
4 75 ____________
5 100 ____________

☐ / 5

2 Look at the pictures and write the words.

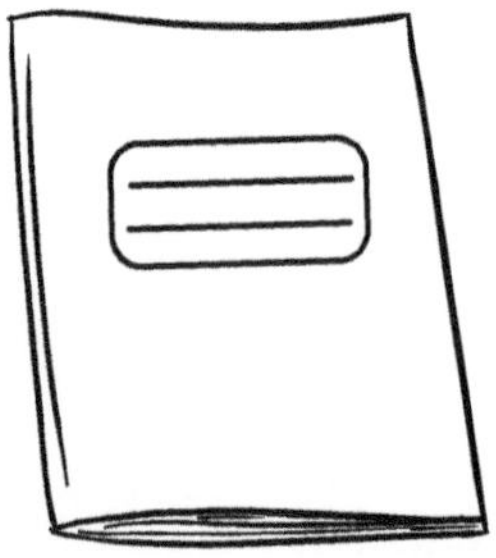

0 n *o t e b o o k*

1 c _ _ c _

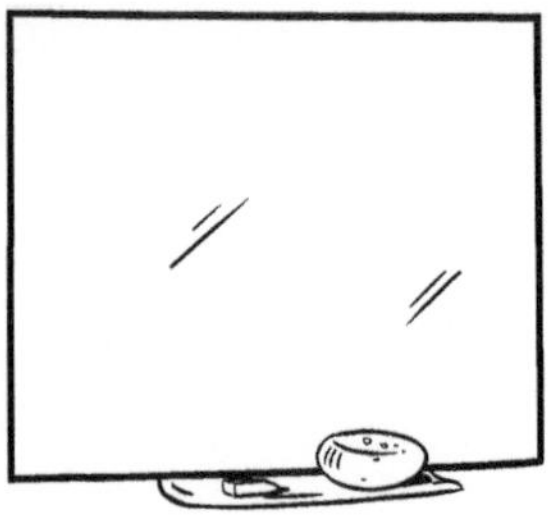

2 b _ a _ _

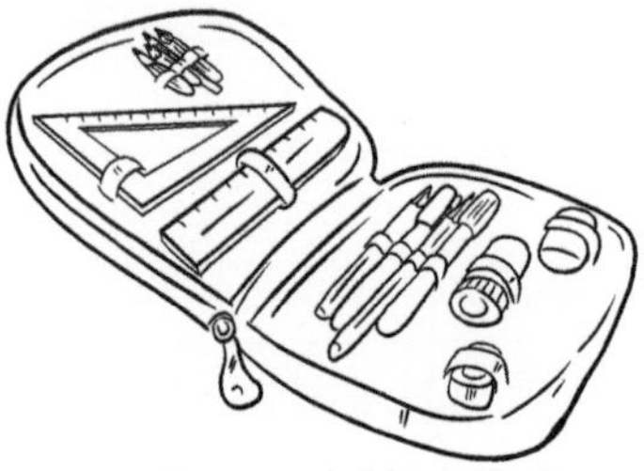

3 p _ _ _ _ l c _ _ _

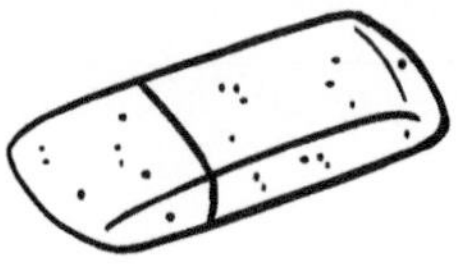

4 r _ _ _ _ r

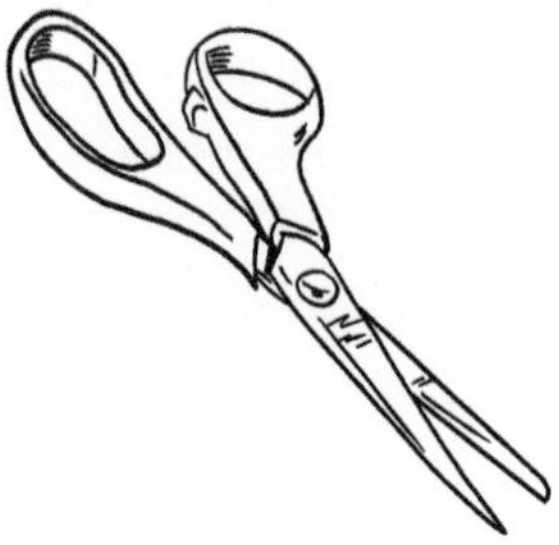

5 s _ _ _ s _ _ _

☐ / 5

3 Complete the sentences with the words in the box. There is one extra word.

black blue green grey pink ~~purple~~ yellow

0 Lavender is *purple*.
1 Zebras are ____________ and white.
2 Trees are ____________.
3 Lemons are ____________.
4 Flamingos are ____________.
5 Elephants are ____________.

☐ / 5

Grammar

4 Circle the correct word.

0 It's (a) / *an* cupcake.
1 It's *a* / *an* elephant.
2 It's *a* / *an* zebra.
3 It's *a* / *an* flower.
4 It's *a* / *an* orange.
5 It's *a* / *an* umbrella.

☐ / 5

5 Write sentences. Use plural forms.

0 It's a coloured pencil.
They're coloured pencils.
1 It's a sandwich.
____
2 It's a pencil case.
____
3 It's an orange.
____
4 It's a box.
____
5 It's a desk.
____

☐ / 5

Communication

6 Match beginnings 1–5 and endings a–e.

0 I'm eleven years [*f*]
1 Sit ☐
2 How do you ☐
3 Can ☐
4 Stand ☐
5 Close ☐

a down.
b you help me?
c spell that?
d your books, please.
e up, please.
f old.

☐ / 5

Vocabulary	☐ / 15	Communication	☐ / 5
Grammar	☐ / 10	**Your total score**	☐ / 30

name ______________________ class ______

Vocabulary

1 Write the numbers.

0 8 *eight*
1 12 ______
2 67 ______
3 14 ______
4 46 ______
5 100 ______

☐ / 5

2 Look at the pictures and write the words.

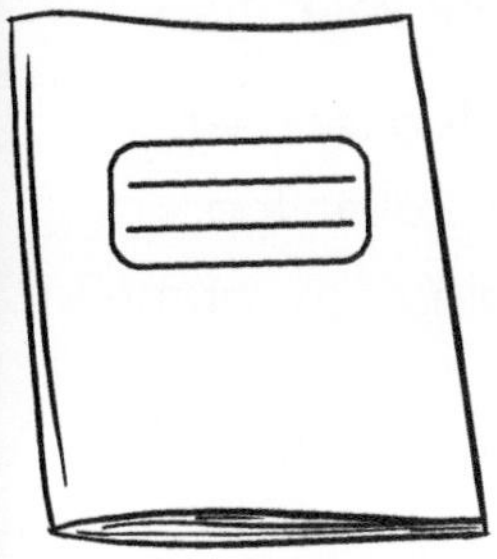

0 n *o t e b o o k*

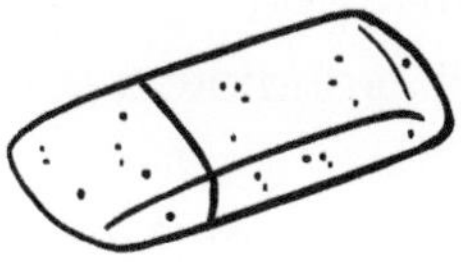

1 r _ b _ _ _

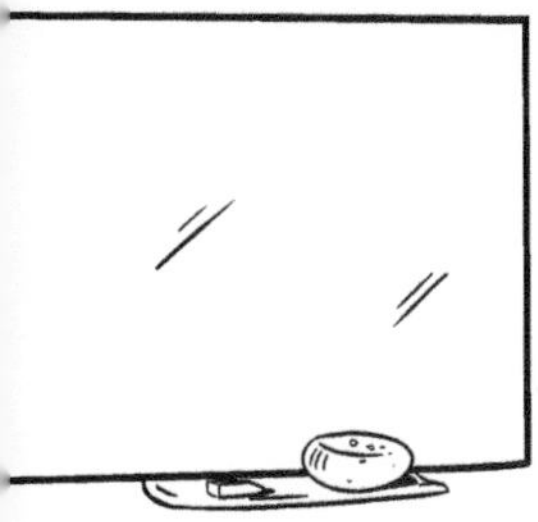

2 b _ _ _ d

3 c _ o _ _

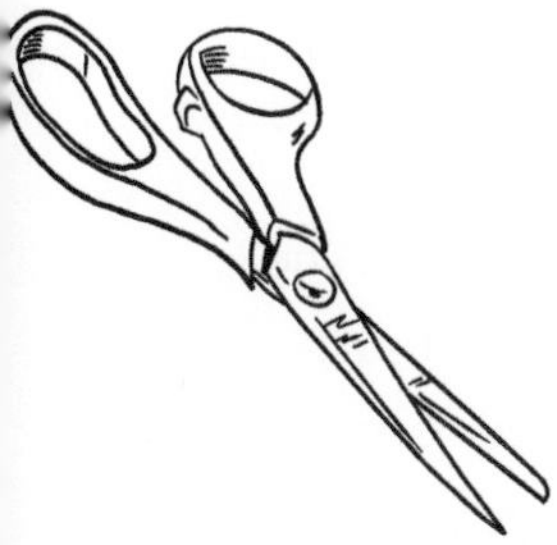

4 s _ _ _ _ _ r _

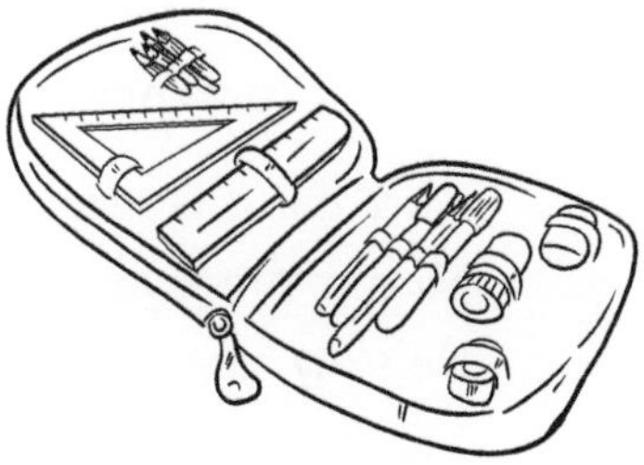

5 p _ _ _ i _ c _ _ _

☐ / 5

3 Complete the sentences with the words in the box. There is one extra word.

blue green grey pink ~~purple~~ white yellow

0 Lavender is *purple*.
1 Elephants are ______.
2 Lemons are ______.
3 Trees are ______.
4 Zebras are black and ______.
5 Flamingos are ______.

☐ / 5

Grammar

4 Circle the correct word.

0 It's (a) / *an* cupcake.
1 It's *a* / *an* flamingo.
2 It's *a* / *an* apple.
3 It's *a* / *an* egg.
4 It's *a* / *an* tree.
5 It's *a* / *an* orange.

☐ / 5

5 Write sentences. Use plural forms.

0 It's a coloured pencil.
They're coloured pencils.
1 It's a computer game.
______
2 It's an umbrella.
______
3 It's a sandwich.
______
4 It's a chair.
______
5 It's a box.
______

☐ / 5

Communication

6 Match beginnings 1–5 and endings a–e.

0 I'm eleven years [*f*]
1 Can ☐
2 What's ☐
3 Stand ☐
4 Open ☐
5 Sit ☐

a down, please.
b you repeat that, please?
c your books.
d your surname?
e up.
f old.

☐ / 5

Vocabulary	☐ / 15	Communication	☐ / 5
Grammar	☐ / 10	**Your total score**	☐ / 30

name _____ class _____

Vocabulary

1 Look at the family tree and complete the sentences.

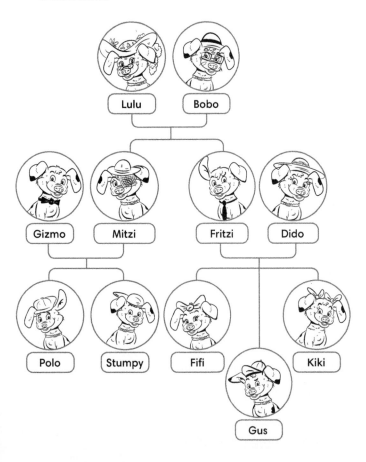

0 Lulu is Gus's _grandmother_.
1 Mitzi is Fifi's _____.
2 Gizmo is Kiki's _____.
3 Polo is Stumpy's _____.
4 Mitzi is Bobo's _____.
5 Gus is Dido's _____.

☐ / 5

2 Complete the sentences with the words in the box. There is one extra word.

> American ~~China~~ on park Poland Polish school UK

Wu and Chen are from ⁰_China_. They're Chinese. They're in the ¹_____.

Jane is British. She's from the ²_____. She's ³_____ holiday.

Mark is from the USA. He's ⁴_____. He's at ⁵_____.

Dorota is from ⁶_____. She's in the garden.

☐ / 6

Grammar

3 Complete the sentences. Write the correct positive [✓] or negative [✗] form of **to be**.

0 My best friend _isn't_ Spanish. ✗
0 My best friend _is_ from Poland. ✓
1 I _____ eleven years old. ✗
2 The man in the photo _____ my dad. ✓
3 You and your family _____ British. ✗
4 Enzo and Maria _____ Italian. ✓
5 His mum _____ a teacher. ✗
6 You and I _____ American. ✓

☐ / 6

4 Complete the sentences with **my**, **your**, **his** or **her**.

0 Stella is a student. _Her_ mum is a teacher.
1 I'm Italian. _____ parents are Italian too.
2 My grandfather is 70 years old. _____ name is Alfie.
3 It's _____ birthday today. Happy birthday!
4 The girl isn't British. _____ nationality is Spanish.

☐ / 4

5 Look at the family tree in Exercise 1. Write sentences with possessive **'s**.

0 Bobo / Fritzi dad _Bobo is Fritzi's dad._
1 Gus mum / Dido
_____
2 Fifi / Kiki sister
_____
3 Fifi cousins / Stumpy and Polo
_____
4 Gizmo and Mitzi / Polo parents
_____

☐ / 4

Communication

6 Number the sentences to make a dialogue.

[1] Dad, this is Gordon.
[ ] Nice to meet you too.
[ ] He's my classmate.
[ ] Nice to meet you.
[ ] Gordon, this is my dad.
[ ] Hello, Gordon.

☐ / 5

| Vocabulary ☐ / 11 | Communication ☐ / 5 |
| Grammar ☐ / 14 | **Your total score** ☐ / 30 |

Language Test B

name ______________________ class ______

Vocabulary

1 Look at the family tree and complete the sentences.

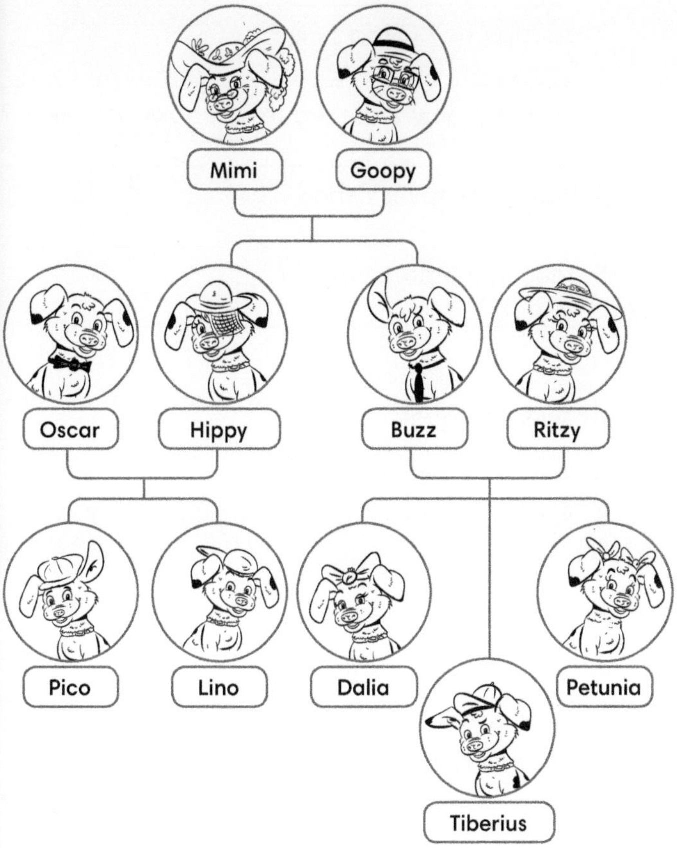

0 Mimi is Pico's *grandmother*.
1 Hippy is Petunia's ______________.
2 Oscar is Tiberius's ______________.
3 Buzz is Hippy's ______________.
4 Petunia is Ritzy's ______________.
5 Lino is Oscar's ______________.

☐ / 5

2 Complete the sentences with the words in the box. There is one extra word.

American British ~~China~~ France French home in on

Li and Chen are from [0]*China*. They're Chinese. They're at [1]__________.

Hank and Carlos are from the USA. They're [2]__________. They're [3]__________ holiday.

Sharon is [4]__________. She's from the UK. She's [5]__________ the garden.

Celine is from [6]__________. She's in the park.

☐ / 6

Grammar

3 Complete the sentences. Write the correct positive [✓] or negative [✗] form of *to be*.

0 My best friend *isn't* Spanish. ✗
0 My best friend *is* from Poland. ✓
1 You and your friends __________ Polish. ✗
2 The superhero in the photo __________ Dug. ✓
3 My sister and I __________ at school. ✓
4 I __________ from Italy. ✗
5 Her dad __________ a teacher. ✗
6 Juan and Dolores __________ Spanish. ✓

☐ / 6

4 Complete the sentences with *my*, *your*, *his* or *her*.

0 Stella is a student. *Her* mum is a teacher.
1 Hi, Jane! It's _____ birthday today. Happy birthday!
2 I'm Polish. _____ friends are Polish too.
3 The boy isn't American. _____ nationality is Italian.
4 My granny is 67 years old. _____ name is Annabella.

☐ / 4

5 Look at the family tree in Exercise 1. Write sentences with possessive *'s*.

0 Goopy / Buzz dad *Goopy is Buzz's dad.*
1 Lino mum / Hippy
____
2 Dalia / Petunia sister
____
3 Pico cousins / Dalia, Petunia and Tiberius
____
4 Oscar and Hippy / Lino parents
____

☐ / 4

Communication

6 Number the sentences to make a dialogue.

[*1*] Mum, this is Ivy.
[ ] Hello, Ivy.
[ ] Nice to meet you too.
[ ] Nice to meet you.
[ ] Ivy, this is my mum.
[ ] She's my friend.

☐ / 5

Vocabulary	☐ / 11	Communication	☐ / 5
Grammar	☐ / 14	**Your total score**	☐ / 30

name ______________________ class ________

Vocabulary

1 Look at the picture. Complete the words.

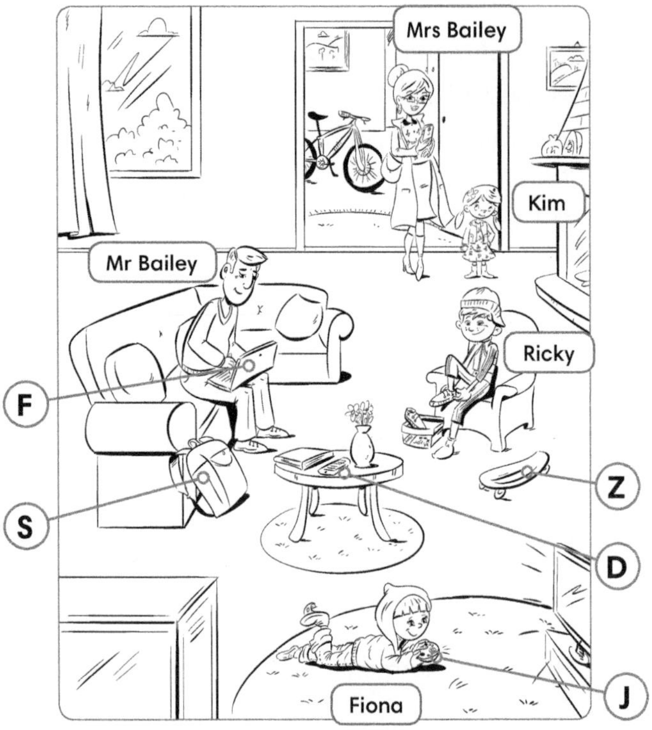

Mrs Bailey 's [0]**t** _o_ **p** is black and white. Her [1]**s** _ _ _ **t** and her coat are long, but they aren't too long. Kim's dress is blue. Her jacket is [2]**s** _ _ _ **t**. Mr Bailey's shoes, [3]**j** _ _ _ _ **r** and trousers aren't cool. They're [4]**b** _ _ _ _ **g**. Fiona's hoodie is [5]**t** _ **o** big. Her shoes are old and her jeans are too long. Ricky's cap is green. His [6]**t** _ _ _ _ _ _ _ **t** is brown, but it's too small. His trainers are [7]**n** _ **w**.

☐ / [7]

2 Look at the picture in Exercise 1. Write the words.

0 F is a _laptop_ _computer_.
1 J is a __________ __________.
2 D is a __________ __________.
3 Z is a ____________________.
4 S is a ____________________.

☐ / [4]

Grammar

3 Write *this*, *that*, *these* or *those* in the sentences.

0 _This_ is your T-shirt. ⇒
1 _____ are my hoodies. ⇒
2 _____ jeans aren't old. ⇒
3 _____ cap isn't Andy's. ⇒
4 _____ top is Mum's. ⇒

☐ / [4]

4 Write questions.

0 is / old / it / too / ? _Is it too old?_
1 they / best friends / are / ?
____
2 cousin / he / Olivia's / is / ?
____
3 for me / new / are / comic books / those / ?
____
4 from / where / is / she / ?
____
5 you / in the park / are / ?
____

☐ / [5]

5 Answer the questions.

A: Are those hoodies cool?
B: [0]_Yes, they are._ ✓ **B:** [0]_No, they aren't._ ✗
A: Is Nicolas in the garden?
B: [1] ____________________ ✗
A: Is the suit too old?
B: [2] ____________________ ✓
A: Are you and your sister happy?
B: [3] ____________________ ✗
A: Are these trousers too long?
B: [4] ____________________ ✓
A: Is your mum Spanish?
B: [5] ____________________ ✓

☐ / [5]

Communication

6 Complete the dialogue with one word in each gap.

Harry: Hi. [0]**W**_hat_'s your name?
Mia: My name's Mia.
Harry: [1]**W**__________ are you from, Mia?
Mia: I'm from Rome. I'm Italian.
Harry: How [2]**o**__________ are you?
Mia: I'm eleven [3]**y**__________ old.
Harry: [4]**W**__________'s your favourite actor?
Mia: Good question. Ryan Gosling.
Harry: And [5]**w**__________'s your favourite film?
Mia: _The Jungle Book_. It's fantastic.
Harry: It's my favourite film too.

☐ / [5]

Vocabulary	☐ / [11]	Communication	☐ / [5]
Grammar	☐ / [14]	**Your total score**	☐ / [30]

2 Language Test B

name ______________________ class ________

Vocabulary

1 Look at the picture. Complete the words.

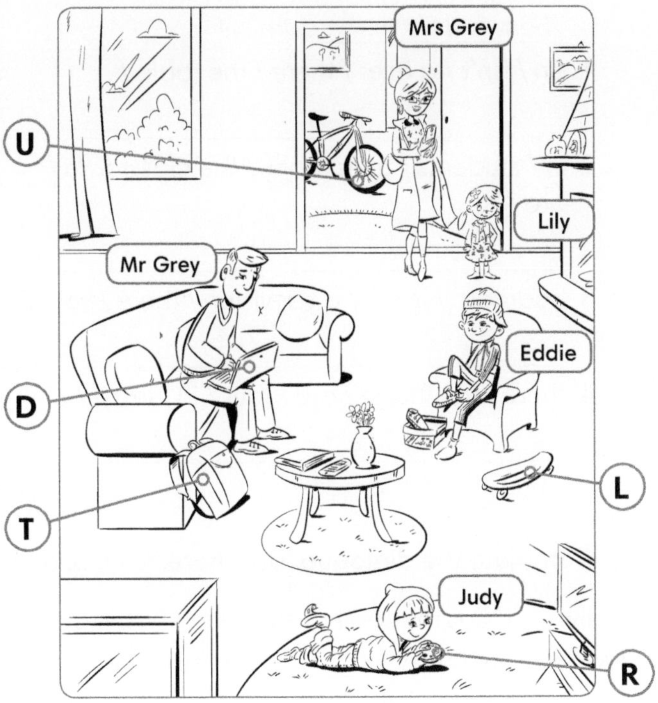

Mr Grey's [0]**s** _h o e_ **s**, jumper and trousers are boring. They aren't [1]**c** _ _ **l**. Judy's [2]**h** _ _ _ _ **e** is too big. Her shoes are too [3]**o** _ **d** and her jeans are too long. Eddie's cap is red. His tracksuit is blue, but it's [4]**t** _ **o** small. His [5]**t** _ _ _ _ _ _ **s** are new. Lily's dress is pink. Her short [6]**j** _ _ _ _ **t** is pink too. Mrs Grey's top is black and white. Her coat and her [7]**s** _ _ _ **t** are long, but they aren't too long.

☐ / 7

2 Look at the picture in Exercise 1. Write the words.

0 D is a _laptop_ _computer_.
1 U is a __________ __________.
2 T is a ____________________.
3 R is a __________ __________.
4 L is a ____________________.

☐ / 4

Grammar

3 Write *this*, *that*, *these* or *those* in the sentences.

0 _This_ is your T-shirt.
1 _____ suit isn't John's.
2 _____ are his trainers.
3 _____ trousers aren't old.
4 _____ dress is Lucy's.

☐ / 4

4 Write questions.

0 is / old / it / too / ? _Is it too old?_
1 how / is / he / old / ?
____
2 good / they / students / are / ?
____
3 you / in / the garden / are / ?
____
4 these / for me / old / are / comic books / ?
____
5 aunt / she / Joe's / is / ?
____

☐ / 5

5 Answer the questions.

A: Are those hoodies cool?
B: [0]_Yes, they are._ ✓ **B:** [0]_No, they aren't._ ✗
A: Are you and your best friend on holiday?
B: [1]____________________ ✓
A: Is her dad Italian?
B: [2]____________________ ✗
A: Are those shoes too small for you?
B: [3]____________________ ✗
A: Is Helen at home?
B: [4]____________________ ✓
A: Is the jacket too long?
B: [5]____________________ ✗

☐ / 5

Communication

6 Complete the dialogue with one word in each gap.

Ann: Hi. [0]**W**_hat_'s your name?
Claude: Claude. Claude Dubois.
Ann: How [1]**o**__________ are you, Claude?
Claude: I'm twelve [2]**y**__________ old.
Ann: I'm eleven. Where are you [3]**f**__________?
Claude: Paris. I'm French.
Ann: [4]**W**__________ are your favourite sports?
Claude: Football and tennis.
Ann: [5]**W**__________'s your favourite sports person?
Claude: Roger Federer. He's fantastic!
Ann: High five! He's my favourite sports person too.

☐ / 5

Vocabulary	☐ / 11	Communication	☐ / 5
Grammar	☐ / 14	**Your total score**	☐ / 30

name ______________________ class ______

Vocabulary

1 Look at the picture. Write the words.

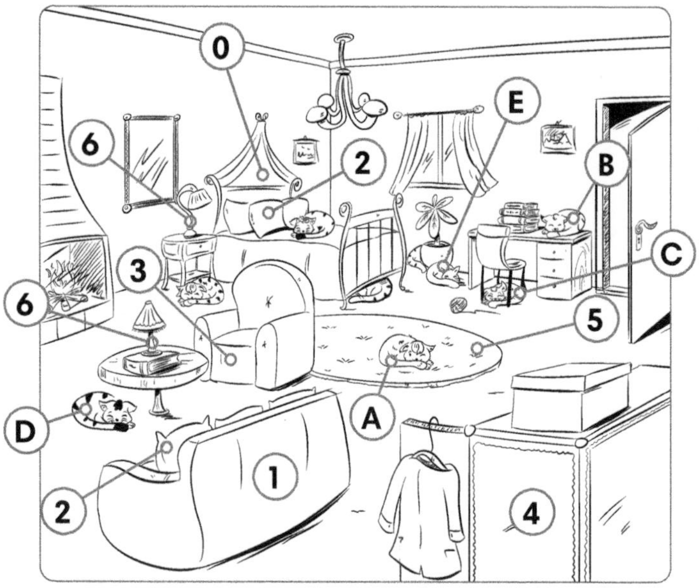

0 b*ed*
1 s__________
2 c__________s
3 a__________
4 w__________
5 c__________
6 l__________s

☐ / 6

2 Look at the picture in Exercise 1. Complete the answers with prepositions of place.

Where's ...?

0 Cat A? It's *in* the bedroom.
1 Cat B? It's __________ the desk.
2 Cat C? It's __________ the chair.
3 Cat D? It's __________ to the table.
4 Cat E? It's __________ of the plant.

☐ / 4

Grammar

3 Complete the sentences. Use *there is / there are* in the positive [✓], negative [✗] or question [?] form.

0 *There is* a table in the kitchen. ✓
0 *There isn't* a table in the kitchen. ✗
0 *Is there* a table in the kitchen? ?
1 __________ twenty chairs in the classroom. ✓
2 __________ a phone on the table? ?
3 __________ two beds in the bedroom. ✗
4 __________ a desk in the bedroom. ✓
5 __________ a rat behind the door. ✗
6 __________ four people at home? ?

☐ / 6

4 Make positive sentences, negative sentences or questions.

0 there / is / the garage / a rat / in / !
There is a rat in the garage!
1 on / isn't / a ruler / there / the table / .
____
2 in / students / there / any / the classroom / are / ?
____
3 bedroom / is / in / a television / there / your / ?
____
4 there / the fridge / are / four / in / eggs / .
____

☐ / 4

5 Complete the dialogue. Use *there*, *isn't*, *a*, *any*.

Sally: This is my new house. There's 0*a* big garden.
Marina: Are there 1__________ trees in the garden?
Sally: No, there aren't 2__________ trees. The garden is too small for trees. But the house is big.
Marina: Is your bedroom big?
Sally: Yes, it is. There's a bed, a desk and a chair. 3__________ are four posters on the wall too.
Marina: Is there 4__________ games console?
Sally: No, there 5__________, but there's a computer!

☐ / 5

Communication

6 Complete the dialogue with the words in the box. There is one extra word.

~~come~~ let please upstairs what's where's would

A: Hello. Please 0*come* in.
B: Thank you.
A: 1__________ you like a sandwich?
B: Yes, 2__________. 3__________ the bathroom, please?
A: It's 4__________. It's next to Andrew's bedroom. 5__________ me show you.
B: Thanks.

☐ / 5

Vocabulary	☐ / 10	Communication	☐ / 5
Grammar	☐ / 15	**Your total score**	☐ / 30

name _____ class _____

Vocabulary

1 Look at the picture. Write the words.

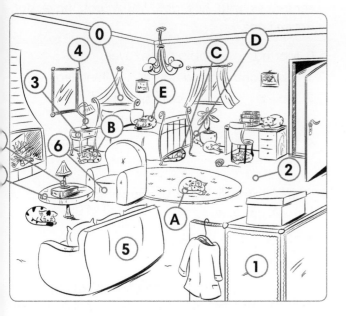

0 b<u>ed</u>
1 w_____
2 f_____
3 t_____s
4 l_____s
5 s_____
6 a_____

☐ / 6

2 Look at the picture in Exercise 1. Complete the answers with prepositions of place.

Where's ...?

0 Cat A? It's *in* the bedroom.
1 Cat B? It's _____ to the table.
2 Cat C? It's _____ the bed.
3 Cat D? It's _____ the plant.
4 Cat E? It's _____ the bed.

☐ / 4

Grammar

3 Complete the sentences. Use *there is / there are* in the positive [✓], negative [✗] or question [?] form.

0 *There is* a table in the kitchen. ✓
0 *There isn't* a table in the kitchen. ✗
0 *Is there* a table in the kitchen? ?
1 _____ a chair in the classroom. ✗
2 _____ three girls in your family? ?
3 _____ ten computers in the classroom. ✗
4 _____ a carton of milk in the kitchen. ✓
5 _____ a dog under the table? ?
6 _____ two wardrobes in the bedroom. ✓

☐ / 6

4 Make positive sentences, negative sentences or questions.

0 there / is / the garage / a rat / in / !
   There is a rat in the garage!
1 in / isn't / a pencil / there / the pencil case / .

   _____

2 the living room / is / in / a games console / there / ?

   _____

3 there / the tree / aren't / any / on / apples / .

   _____

4 in / oranges / there / any / the kitchen / are / ?

   _____

☐ / 4

5 Complete the dialogue. Use *there, are, a, any*.

Lily: This is my new house. There's ⁰<u>a</u> big garden.
Kate: Are there ¹_____ plants in the garden?
Lily: Yes, there ²_____, but there isn't a table and there aren't ³_____ chairs.
Kate: Is your bedroom big?
Lily: Yes, it is. There's a bed, a desk and a chair, and ⁴_____ are three posters on the wall.
Kate: Is there ⁵_____ wardrobe?
Lily: Yes, there is and there's a carpet too.

☐ / 5

Communication

6 Complete the dialogue with the words in the box. There is one extra word.

downstairs   like   ~~please~~   show   thank   what's   where's

A: Hello. ⁰<u>Please</u> come in.
B: Thank you.
A: Would you ¹_____ a sandwich?
B: No, ²_____ you. ³_____ the bathroom, please?
A: It's ⁴_____. It's next to my bedroom. Let me ⁵_____ you.
B: Thanks.

☐ / 5

Vocabulary ☐ / 10   Communication ☐ / 5
Grammar ☐ / 15   **Your total score** ☐ / 30

name _____ class _____

Vocabulary

1 Look at the picture and complete the text with the words in the box. There is one extra word.

> ears feet fingers hands ~~head~~ legs neck toes

Martha's **0**_head_ is big and her **1**_____ is long. Her body is small and her **2**_____ are short. There are twelve **3**_____ on her **4**_____ and there are six **5**_____ on her **6**_____.

◯ / 6

2 Complete the words in the sentences with the groups of letters in the box. There is one extra group.

> ce ~~ful~~ ly ny ty ver

0 She's **help**_ful_ and she helps her friend with her homework.
1 He likes tennis and taekwondo. He's **spor**___.
2 She's very **ni**___. She's got a cool present for her dad.
3 He's a good student. He's **cle**___.
4 She's **fun**___ and she tells great jokes.

◯ / 4

Grammar

3 Look at the picture in Exercise 1. Complete the sentences *with has got, hasn't got, have got, haven't got.*

0 Martha _has got_ big brown eyes.
1 Albert and Martha _____ long legs.
2 Albert _____ dark spiky hair.
3 Martha _____ long curly hair.
4 Harold and Albert _____ blond hair.

◯ / 4

4 Complete the dialogue. Use *has, hasn't, have, haven't, got, they.*

A: **0**_Have_ you got a new robot?
B: Yes, I **1**_____.
A: **2**_____ your brother got a robot too?
B: Yes, he has, but his robot **3**_____ got a battery.
A: Have your parents **4**_____ a robot?
B: No, **5**_____ haven't.
A: And your friends? What **6**_____ they got?
B: They **7**_____ got robots, but they've got super suits.

◯ / 7

5 Complete sentence B in each pair. Use *its, their, your, our.*

0 **A** Mike and Veronica have got white teeth.
   B _Their teeth_ are white.
1 **A** My sister and I have got dark blue eyes.
   B _____ are dark blue.
2 **A** The car has got a new battery.
   B _____ is new.
3 **A** You and your parents have got a cool house.
   B _____ is cool.
4 **A** The students have got a great teacher.
   B _____ is great.

◯ / 4

Communication

6 Circle the correct answer in the dialogues.

A: Are you OK?	**A:** **2**Sorry *on / about* that!
B: **0**I'm fine / no.	**B:** **3**That's *all / so* right.
A: **1**I'm *too / so* sorry.	**A:** **4**Sorry, my *wrong / mistake.*
B: It's OK.	**B:** **5***No / Not* problem.

◯ / 5

Vocabulary ◯ / 10		Communication ◯ / 5	
Grammar ◯ / 15		**Your total score** ◯ / 30	

name _____   class _____

Vocabulary

1 Look at the picture and complete the text with the words in the box. There is one extra word.

> body feet fingers hands ~~head~~ mouth
> toes tooth

Martha

Harold

Albert

Harold's **0**_head_ is small. His **1**_____ is big and his legs are long. His **2**_____ is big and he's got one **3**_____. There are six **4**_____ on his feet and there are six **5**_____ on his **6**_____.

◯/ 6

2 Complete the words in the sentences with the groups of letters in the box. There is one extra group.

> ce ~~ful~~ ly ny ty ver

0 She's **help**_ful_ and she helps her friend with her homework.

1 He tells great jokes. He's **fun**__.

2 She's **spor**__. She likes taekwondo and tennis.

3 He's got a great present for his friend. He's very **ni**__.

4 She's **friend**__. She speaks to everyone.

◯/ 4

Grammar

3 Look at the picture in Exercise 1. Complete the sentences *with has got, hasn't got, have got, haven't got.*

0 Martha _has got_ big brown eyes.

1 Albert _____ curly blond hair.

2 Martha and Harold _____ small blue eyes.

3 Albert and Harold _____ short hair.

4 Martha _____ a big mouth.

◯/ 4

4 Complete the dialogue. Use *has, hasn't, have, haven't, got, they.*

A:**0**_Have_ you got a new robot?

B: No, I **1**_____.

A: Have your parents **2**_____ a robot?

B: Yes, **3**_____ have.

A:**4**_____ your sister got a robot too?

B: Yes, but her robot **5**_____ got a battery.

A: What **6**_____ your friends got?

B: They **7**_____ got robots and the robots have got batteries!

◯/ 7

5 Complete sentence B in each pair. Use *its, their, your, our.*

0 A Mike and Veronica have got white teeth.

  B _Their teeth_ are white.

1 A The house has got a big garden.

  B _____ is big.

2 A Rebecca and I have got brown eyes.

  B _____ are brown.

3 A The teachers have got great students.

  B _____ are great.

4 A You and your friends have got good marks.

  B _____ are good.

◯/ 4

Communication

6 Circle the correct answer in the dialogues.

A: Are you OK?	A:**3**Sorry *about* / *on* that!
B:**0**I'm *fine* / *no*.	B:**4**That's *so* / *all* right.
A:**1**Sorry, my *mistake* / *wrong*.	A:**5**I'm *so* / *too* sorry.
	B: It's OK.
B:**2***Not* / *No* problem.	◯/ 5

| Vocabulary ◯/ 10 | Communication ◯/ 5 |
| Grammar ◯/ 15 | **Your total score** ◯/ 30 |

name _____ class _____

Vocabulary

1 Look at the picture and complete the text.

What can they do?

Those birds can ⁰f / y and these birds can ¹s _ _ _.
The cat can ²c _ _ _ _ the tree. The children can
³s _ _ _. The girl can ⁴d _ _ _. The man can
⁵c _ _ _ well. The girl can ⁶j _ _ _.

◯ / 6

2 Complete the text with the words in the box.
There is one extra word.

> draw   fix   ~~make~~   play   play   read   ride

Dad can't ⁰*make* cupcakes but he can
¹_____ cars and bikes. Mum can
²_____ great pictures and she can
³_____ the guitar. I can't ⁴_____
a horse but I can ⁵_____ football.

◯ / 5

Grammar

3 Write sentences with *can* and *can't*.

0 flamingoes / fly *Flamingoes can fly.*
1 elephants / jump _____
2 cats / sing songs _____
3 zebras / run fast _____
4 dogs / climb trees _____

◯ / 4

4 Write questions.

0 camera / fix / you / can / this / ?
Can you fix this camera?
1 here / Freddie / skateboard / can / ?
_____
2 tennis / Marcus / can / play / ?
_____
3 Dave / cook / can / what / ?
_____
4 two / Amy / can / boats / see?
_____

◯ / 4

5 Complete the dialogue. Use *can, can't, what, she.*

A: I ⁰*can't* make pizzas. ¹_____ you help me?
B: No, I ²_____. I'm sorry.
A: ³_____ your little sister draw?
B: Yes, ⁴_____ ⁵_____ but she can't write
well.
A: ⁶_____ can your parents play?
B: They can play golf.

◯ / 6

Communication

6 Complete the dialogue. Use one word in each gap.

A: Let's ⁰d*o* something fun!
B: I ¹a_____. Any ideas?
A: Let's go ²s_____!
B: It's not a good ³i_____. I can't swim.
A: We ⁴c_____ go to the park.
B: Yes, let's do ⁵t_____!

◯ / 5

Vocabulary ◯ / 11	Communication ◯ / 5
Grammar ◯ / 14	**Your total score** ◯ / 30

5 Language Test B

name ______________________ class ______

Vocabulary

1 Look at the picture and complete the text.

What can they do?

The birds can [0]**f** _l y_. The children can [1]**s** _ _ _. This girl can [2]**d** _ _ _ and that girl can [3]**j** _ _ _. The cat can [4]**c** _ _ _ _ the tree. The boys can [5]**s** _ _ _ _ _ _ _ _ _. Those birds can [6]**s** _ _ _.

☐ / 6

2 Complete the text with the words in the box. There is one extra word.

draw	fix	~~make~~	play	play	read	ride

Dad can't [0]_make_ cupcakes but he can [1]__________ great pictures. Mum can't [2]__________ computers but she can [3]__________ the piano. I can't [4]__________ a bike but I can [5]__________ tennis.

☐ / 5

Grammar

3 Write sentences with *can* and *can't*.

0 flamingoes / fly _Flamingoes can fly._
1 cats / climb trees __________
2 elephants / dive __________
3 dogs / sing songs __________
4 zebras / run fast __________

☐ / 4

4 Write questions.

0 camera / fix / you / can / this / ?
Can you fix this camera?
1 play / Freddie / tennis / can / ?
____
2 write / Marcus / what / can / ?
____
3 posters / Sam / can / make / ?
____
4 Barbara / Evan / play / can / and / football?
____

☐ / 4

5 Complete the dialogue. Use *can, can't, what, he*.

A: I [0]_can't_ make cupcakes. [1]__________ you and Henry help me?
B: No, we [2]__________. Sorry.
A: [3]__________ can your friends play?
B: They can play tennis.
A: [4]__________ your little brother draw?
B: Yes, [5]__________ [6]__________ but he can't write well.

☐ / 6

Communication

6 Complete the dialogue. Use one word in each gap.

A: Let's [0]**d**_o_ something fun!
B: I agree. [1]**A**__________ ideas?
A: Let's go [2]**s**__________!
B: It's not a good [3]**i**__________. I can't skateboard.
A: We [4]**c**__________ go to the zoo.
B: Yes, let's [5]**d**__________ that!

☐ / 5

Vocabulary	☐ / 11	Communication	☐ / 5
Grammar	☐ / 14	**Your total score**	☐ / 30

6 Language Test A

name ____________________ class ______

Vocabulary

1 Complete the text with the words in the box. There is one extra word.

dinner do get make ~~Mondays~~ out Saturdays shower to Wednesdays

HOME | ABOUT ME | CONTACT

My daily routine

by Gemma Miles

On [0]*Mondays*, Tuesdays, [1]________, Thursdays and Fridays, I [2]__________ up early and have a [3]__________. Then I have breakfast and I go to school. After school, I [4]__________ my homework. In the evening, I have [5]__________. Then I watch TV or listen [6]__________ music. I go to bed early. On [7]__________ and Sundays I hang [8]__________ with my friends.

☐ / [8]

2 Write the missing months.

January → [0]*February* → March →
[1]______________ → May → [2]______________ →
July → [3]______________ → September →
October → [4]______________ → December

☐ / [4]

Grammar

3 Complete the sentences. Use the Present Simple form of the verbs in the box. There is one extra word.

climb dive draw ~~have~~ play run write

0 We *have* great lessons at school.
1 Sam ____________ football after school.
2 Her friends ____________ great pictures.
3 My sister ____________ fast.
4 You and your brother ____________ stories.
5 His cat ____________ trees.

☐ / [5]

4 Write sentences.

0 I do karate after school.
He *does karate after school.*
1 I have eggs for breakfast.
She ______________________________.
2 I tidy my bedroom every Saturday.
He ______________________________.
3 I watch TV in the evening.
She ______________________________.
4 I fix cars and bikes.
He ______________________________.

☐ / [4]

5 Make sentences. Add the correct adverb of frequency.

Frequency adverbs
****0 always ***00 usually **000 often *0000 sometimes 00000 never

0 I / my / bike / to / ride / school (**000)
I often ride my bike to school.
1 go / to / I / early / on / bed / Monday (****0)
____
2 TV / I / in / watch / the evening (*0000)
____
3 in / cook / breakfast / the morning / I (00000)
____
4 read / in / I / a book / the evening (***00)
____

☐ / [4]

Communication

6 Look at the clocks and answer the questions.

0 What time is the film? — 06:10
It's at ten past six.
1 What time is the match? — 05:30
____
2 What time is our English lesson? — 09:00
____
3 What time is breakfast? — 07:55
____
4 What time is lunch? — 12:45
____
5 What time is bedtime? — 10:15
____

☐ / [5]

Vocabulary	☐ / [12]	Communication	☐ / [5]
Grammar	☐ / [13]	**Your total score**	☐ / [30]

name _____ class _____

Vocabulary

1 Complete the text with the words in the box. There is one extra word.

> breakfast do in ~~Mondays~~ Saturdays
> shower Thursdays to up with

HOME | ABOUT ME | CONTACT

My daily routine

by Gemma Miles

On ⁰*Mondays*, Tuesdays, Wednesdays,
¹_____ and Fridays, I get ²_____
early and I have ³_____. Then I go
to school. After school, I ⁴_____ my
homework. In the evening, I listen ⁵_____
music or watch TV. Then I have a ⁶_____.
I go to bed early. On ⁷_____ and
Sundays I hang out ⁸_____ my friends.

☐ / 8

2 Write the missing months.

January → ⁰*February* → March →
April → ¹_____ → ² _____ →
³_____ → August → September →
⁴_____ → November → December

☐ / 4

Grammar

3 Complete the sentences. Use the Present Simple form of the verbs in the box. There is one extra word.

> climb dive draw ~~have~~ play run write

0 We *have* great lessons at school.
1 You and your sister _____ great stories.
2 Jack's friends _____ good pictures.
3 Anna _____ tennis after school.
4 My cat _____ trees.
5 Her brother _____ fast.

☐ / 5

4 Write sentences.

0 I do karate after school.
He *does karate after school.*
1 I tidy the living room every Saturday.
He _____.
2 I fix bikes and cars.
She _____.
3 I have sandwiches for lunch.
He _____.
4 I watch TV in the evening.
She _____.

☐ / 4

5 Make sentences. Add the correct adverb of frequency.

Frequency adverbs
****0 **always**   ***00 **usually**   **000 **often**
*0000 **sometimes**   00000 **never**

0 I / my / bike / to / ride / school (**000)
I often ride my bike to school.
1 in / cook / dinner / the evening / I (00000)
_____
2 Sunday / go / to / I / late / on / bed (****0)
_____
3 in / read / I / a book / the evening (***00)
_____
4 after / TV / I / watch / school (*0000)
_____

☐ / 4

Communication

6 Look at the clocks and answer the questions.

0 What time is the film?
It's at ten past six.   `06:10`
1 What time is the match?
_____   `04:15`
2 What time is bedtime?
_____   `11:30`
3 What time is our French lesson?
_____   `09:55`
4 What time is dinner?
_____   `05:45`
5 What time is breakfast?
_____   `07:00`

☐ / 5

Vocabulary ☐ / 12	Communication ☐ / 5
Grammar ☐ / 13	**Your total score** ☐ / 30

© Pearson Education Limited 2017 PHOTOCOPIABLE

7 Language Test A

name ______________________ class ________

Vocabulary

1 Complete the text with the words in the box. There is one extra word.

crocodiles cute dangerous flies lions slow snakes ~~strong~~ tortoises ugly

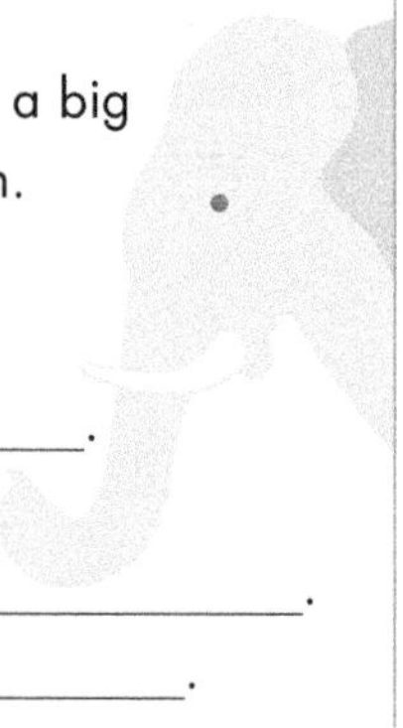

- Elephants are big and 0 *strong*. They've got a long nose and big ears.
- 1 ____________ have got four legs, a big and long mouth and a lot of big teeth. They're 2 ____________.
- 3 ____________ have got four legs. They can't run. They're 4 ____________.
- 5 ____________ have got six legs, two wings and big eyes. They're 6 ____________.
- Baby 7 ____________ are 8 ____________. They've got yellow eyes and big feet.

☐ / 8

2 Look at the pictures and complete the sentences with the names of the animals.

0 It can fly but it can't talk. It's a *parrot*.

1 It can swim and jump. It's a ____________.

2 It can climb trees and it's got four legs. It's a ____________.

3 It's got eight legs. It's small but it can run fast. It's a ____________.

4 It's a good pet and it's got long ears. It's a ____________.

☐ / 4

Grammar

3 Complete the sentences with the negative form of the Present Simple.

0 I *don't like* snakes and spiders. (like)
1 Small dogs ____________ a lot. (eat)
2 Diana ____________ to school. She's nineteen years old. (go)
3 Jake ____________ his homework on Saturdays. He does it on Sundays. (do)
4 Linda and Gordon ____________ TV in the evening. (watch)

☐ / 4

4 Write the questions.

0 A: *Do you want* a dog?
B: Yes, I want a dog.
0 A: *What do you* like?
B: I like animals.
1 A: ____________ early in the morning?
B: No, my sister doesn't get up early in the morning.
2 A: ____________ in the afternoon?
B: Yes, the children have lessons in the afternoon.
3 A: ____________ in the evening?
B: I watch TV in the evening.
4 A: ____________ draw?
B: He draws pictures of animals.

☐ / 4

5 Complete the dialogue with the correct form of the Present Simple.

Kim: Hi, Gerry. Tell me about your weekend. 0 *Do you get up* (you / get up) early?
Gerry: Yes, I 1 ____________ and I make breakfast for the family.
Kim: And your sister Martha?
Gerry: Martha 2 ____________ (not cook) but she helps Dad in the garden. That's a big job! I 3 ____________ (not help) Dad but I help Mum in the house.
Kim: What 4 ____________ (you / do) to relax?
Gerry: I play tennis with my friends.
Kim: 5 ____________ (Martha / play) tennis too?
Martha: No, she doesn't. She plays football.

☐ / 5

Communication

6 Circle the correct answers.

A: 0 *Get* / *Got* your ticket, Petra. Richard and I have got our tickets.
B: 1 *Do* / *Can* I help you?
C: Can I 2 *have* / *take* one ticket to the museum, please?
B: 3 *They're* / *That's* four pounds, please.
C: Here 4 *we* / *you* are.
B: And 5 *here's* / *it's* your ticket.
C: Thanks.

☐ / 5

Vocabulary	☐ / 12	Communication	☐ / 5
Grammar	☐ / 13	**Your total score**	☐ / 30

name _____ class _____

Vocabulary

1 Complete the text with the words in the box. There is one extra word.

> crocodiles cute dangerous flies lions
> slow snakes ~~strong~~ tortoises ugly

- Elephants are big and **0**_strong_. They've got a long nose and big ears.
- **1** _____ can walk but they can't run. They're **2** _____.
- **3** _____ have got four legs, a big and long mouth and a lot of big teeth. They're **4** _____.
- Baby **5** _____ have got yellow eyes and big feet. They're **6** _____.
- **7** _____ have got six legs, two wings and big eyes. They're **8** _____.

◯ / 8

2 Look at the pictures and complete the sentences with the names of the animals.

- **0** It can fly but it can't talk. It's a _parrot_.
- **1** It can climb trees and it's got four legs. It's a _____.
- **2** It's a good pet and it's got long ears. It's a _____.
- **3** It can swim and jump. It's a _____.
- **4** It's got eight legs. It's small but it can run fast. It's a _____.

◯ / 4

Grammar

3 Complete the sentences with the negative form of the Present Simple.

- **0** I _don't like_ snakes and spiders. (like)
- **1** Thomas _____ to school on Saturdays. (go)
- **2** Steve and Gloria _____ to music in the evening. (listen)
- **3** Emma _____ a bike to school. She walks. (ride)
- **4** Cats _____ a lot. (eat)

◯ / 4

4 Write the questions.

- **0** A: _Do you want_ a dog?
  B: _Yes_, I want a dog.
- **0** A: _What do you_ like?
  B: I like _animals_.
- **1** A: _____ at twelve o'clock?
  B: _No_, the students don't have lunch at twelve o'clock.
- **2** A: _____ early on Sundays?
  B: _Yes_, Lucy goes to bed early on Sundays.
- **3** A: _____ draw?
  B: I draw _pictures of flowers_.
- **4** A: _____ in the evening?
  B: _She watches TV_ in the evening.

◯ / 4

5 Complete the dialogue with the correct form of the Present Simple.

Rob: Hi, Ewa. Tell me about your weekend. **0**_Do you get up_ (you / get up) early?

Ewa: No, I **1**_____ but I make lunch for the family.

Rob: And your brother Zac?

Ewa: Zac **2**_____ (not cook) but he helps Dad in the garden. That's a big job! I **3**_____ (not help) Dad but I help Mum in the house.

Rob: What **4**_____ (you / do) to relax?

Ewa: I play computer games with my friends.

Rob: **5**_____ (Zac / play) computer games too?

Martha: Yes, he does.

◯ / 5

Communication

6 Circle the correct answers.

A: (**0**_Get_) / _Got_ your ticket, Petra. Richard and I have got our tickets.

B: **1**_Can / Do_ I help you?

C: Can I **2**_take / have_ one ticket to the museum, please?

B: **3**_That's / They're_ four pounds, please.

C: Here **4**_you / we_ are.

B: And **5**_it's / here's_ your ticket.

C: Thanks.

◯ / 5

Vocabulary ◯ / 12	Communication ◯ / 5
Grammar ◯ / 13	**Your total score** ◯ / 30

8 Language Test A

name _____ class _____

Vocabulary

1 Complete the text with the words in the box. There is one extra word.

cycling   does   goes   hockey   plays   sailing   skiing   ~~swimming~~

Hi Anna!
My family and I love sports. We go ⁰*swimming* in the summer and we go ¹_____ in the winter. I love outdoor sports and I play ²_____ and football. My sister likes indoor sports and she ³_____ taekwondo. My brother ⁴_____ tennis and he goes ⁵_____ on his mountain bike. My mum and dad go ⁶_____ when the weather is good.
What about you and your family?
Sally

☐/ 6

2 Circle the correct answer.

Do you want to be healthy?

✔ Do you ⁰_____ your teeth after meals?
✔ Do you ¹_____ some exercise every day? It's good to be active.
✔ Do you ²___ a lot of water and ³_____ fruit and vegetables?
✔ Do you usually go ⁴_____ bed early?
✔ Do you ⁵_____ friends? It's good to hang out with people you love.

0 a wash	ⓑ brush	3 a eat	b make
1 a have	b do	4 a at	b to
2 a dive	b drink	5 a have	b do

☐/ 5

Grammar

3 Complete the dialogue with the correct form of the verbs.

A: What do you do in the summer holidays?
B: My brother and I like ⁰*swimming* (swim). We ⁰*love* (love) sailing too.
A: What about your mum?
B: My mum ¹_____ (not like) sitting on the beach. She likes ²_____ (go) to museums. She ³_____ (love) walking too.
A: And your dad?
B: Dad hates the beach and he hates ⁴_____ (get) wet!

☐/ 4

4 Complete the sentences with *me, it, her, us, them*.

0 You're my best friend and I love *you*.
1 That's a great mountain bike. I want _____!
2 Gina and Gino are good at dancing. Let's watch _____.
3 Elaine is behind the door. I can't see _____.
4 My sister and I love Mum and Dad and they love _____.
5 I can sing. Listen to _____!

☐/ 5

5 Write the questions. Use the question words in the box.

~~how many~~   what   when   where   who   whose

0 A: *How many brothers have you got?*
   B: I've got <u>two</u> brothers.
1 A: _____
   B: She has lunch <u>at one o'clock</u>.
2 A: _____
   B: Henry wants to go <u>to France</u>.
3 A: _____
   B: My favourite colour is <u>green</u>.
4 A: _____
   B: I love <u>my family and friends</u>.
5 A: _____
   B: It's <u>Janice's</u> horse.

☐/ 5

Communication

6 Look at the pictures and complete the text.

What's the weather like in Spain?

It's ⁰*hot* and
¹_____ in summer. It's
²_____ and
³_____ in autumn. It's
⁴_____ and
⁵_____ in winter.
It's warm in spring.

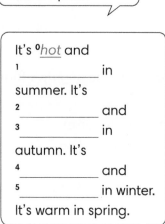

☐/ 5

| Vocabulary ☐/ ⑪ | Communication ☐/ ⑤ |
| Grammar ☐/ ⑭ | **Your total score** ☐/ ㉚ |

name _____ class _____

Vocabulary

1 Complete the text with the words in the box. There is one extra word.

> cycling does goes hockey plays sailing
> skiing ~~swimming~~

Hi Anna!
My family and I love sports. We go **0**_swimming_ in the summer and we go **1**_____ in the winter. My brother likes indoor sports and he **2**_____ taekwondo. My sister goes **3**_____ on her mountain bike and she **4**_____ tennis. My mum and dad go **5**_____ when the weather is good. I love outdoor sports and I play **6**_____ and football.
What about you and your family?
Sally

☐ / 6

2 Circle the correct answer.

Do you want to be healthy?

✔ Do you **0**_____ your teeth after meals?
✔ Do you usually go **1**_____ bed early?
✔ Do you **2**_____ fruit and vegetables and **3**_____ a lot of water?
✔ Do you **4**_____ some exercise every day? It's good to be active.
✔ Do you **5**_____ friends? It's good to hang out with people you love.

0	a wash	(b) brush	3 a dive	b drink
1	a to	b in	4 a do	b have
2	a make	b eat	5 a have	b do

☐ / 5

Grammar

3 Complete the dialogue with the correct form of the verbs.

A: What do you do in the summer holidays?

B: Lisa and I love **0**_swimming_ (swim). We **0**_like_ (like) sailing too.

A: What about your mum?

B: My mum likes **1**_____ (go) to museums. She **2**_____ (love) walking too. She hates **3**_____ (sit) on the beach.

A: And your dad?

B: Dad hates the beach and he **4**_____ (not like) getting wet!

☐ / 4

4 Complete the sentences with it, us, him, them, her.

0 You're my best friend and I love _you_.
1 Dave is behind the door. You can't see _____.
2 Kate can play the guitar. Listen to _____.
3 This hoodie is cool. Look at _____.
4 The children love their parents and their parents love _____.
5 We're good at acting. Watch _____!

☐ / 5

5 Write the questions. Use the question words in the box.

> ~~how many~~ what when where who whose

0 A: _How many brothers have you got?_
   B: I've got <u>two</u> brothers.
1 A: _____
   B: He loves <u>his grandad and granny</u>.
2 A: _____
   B: Our favourite colour is <u>yellow</u>.
3 A: _____
   B: They're <u>Ursula's</u> dogs.
4 A: _____
   B: I live <u>in Rome</u>.
5 A: _____
   B: They usually have breakfast <u>at seven o'clock</u>.

☐ / 5

Communication

6 Look at the pictures and complete the text.

What's the weather like in Italy?

It's **0**_cold_ and **1**_____ in winter. It's warm in spring. It's **2**_____ and **3**_____ in summer. It's **4**_____ and **5**_____ in autumn.

☐ / 5

Vocabulary ☐ / 11		Communication ☐ / 5	
Grammar ☐ / 14		**Your total score** ☐ / 30	

Skills Test A

name ______________________ class ______

Listening

1 🔊 2 Listen and write *T* (true) or *F* (false).

0 Dan is Mateo's new neighbour. [*T*]
1 Gabriella is Italian. [ ]
2 Mateo is twelve years old. [ ]
3 Peter is from the UK. [ ]
4 Anna is Chinese. [ ]
5 Anna's mother is Chinese. [ ]

[ ] / [5]

2 🔊 3 Listen and complete the sentences with one word.

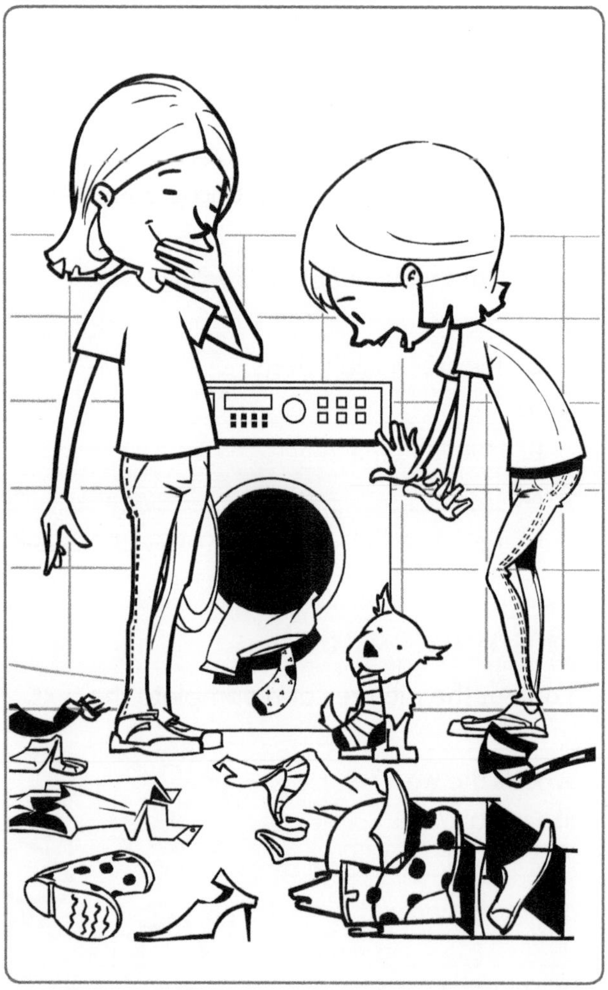

0 The boots are too *big*.
1 Granny's brown coat is __________.
2 The __________ is pink and white.
3 The red and purple hoodie is __________.
4 The new __________ are too long.
5 The girl's favourite colour is __________.

[ ] / [5]

Communication

3 Look at the pictures. Match sentences a–g with situations 1–5. There are two extra sentences.

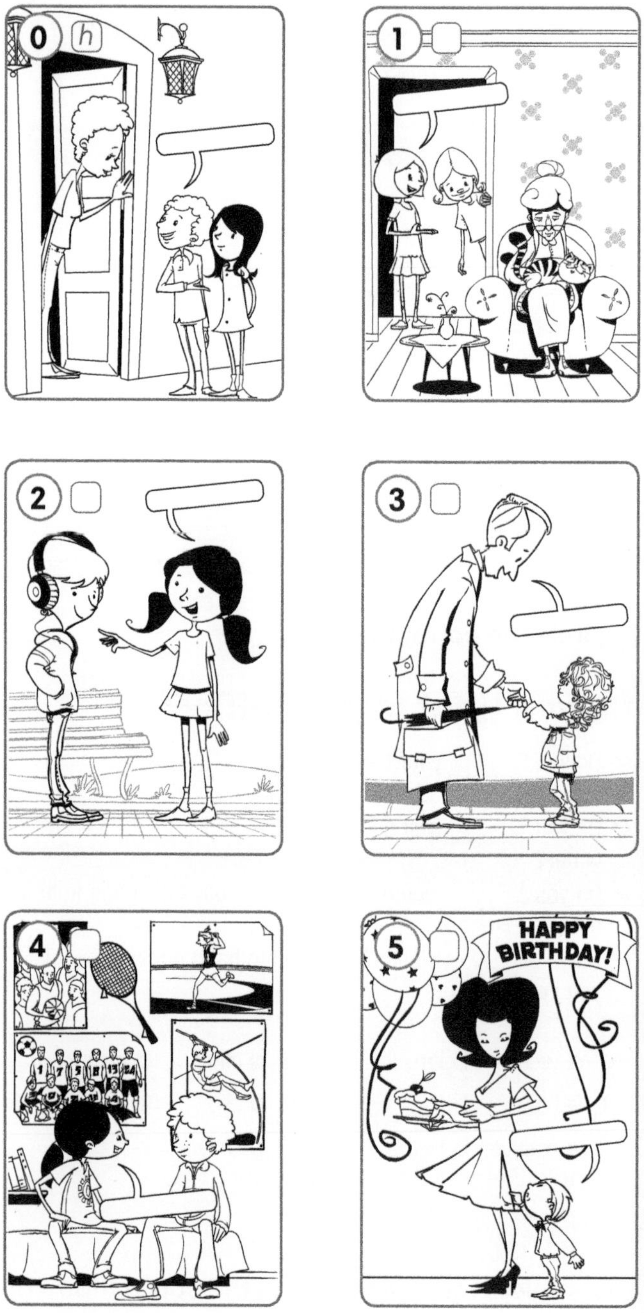
0 *h*
1
2
3
4
5
HAPPY BIRTHDAY!

a How old are you?
b Who's your favourite sports person?
c Nice to meet you too.
d What's your favourite music?
e She's my granny.
f What's 'kino' in English?
g Where are you from?
h Mum, this is Nadia. She's my classmate.

[ ] / [5]

&2 Skills Test A

name ____________________ class ____________________

Reading

4 Read the text. Then read the sentences and write *yes* or *no*.

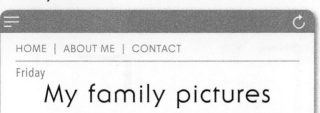

HOME | ABOUT ME | CONTACT

Friday

My family pictures

by Miguel Sanchez

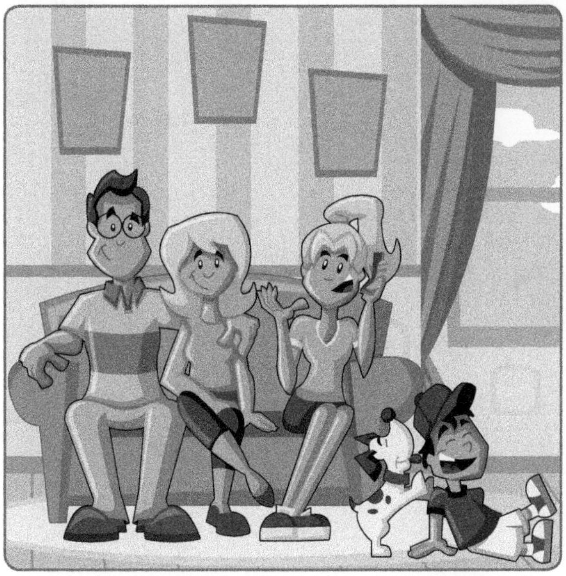

Look at the people in the picture. They're at home. The girl's name is Juana. She's eleven. I'm eleven too. Juana is my cousin *and* my best friend. Her brother, Pedro, is eight. Juana's mum and dad are my aunt and uncle. Uncle Diego is Spanish but Aunt Jeanette is from France. They're teachers.

Uncle Diego's hobby is his garden and Aunt Jeanette loves her pet dog, Plon-Plon. Juana's favourite thing is her cool new mountain bike and Pedro's favourite thing is his little piano. He's a good pianist.

0 The people are at home. *yes*
1 Juana is Miguel's cousin. ______
2 Pedro is Juana's cousin. ______
3 Diego is from France. ______
4 Plon-Plon is Jeanette's dog. ______
5 Juana's bike is new. ______

[ ] / [5]

5 Complete the text with the words in the box. There is one extra word.

are aren't dress from her party ~~those~~

HOME | ABOUT ME | CONTACT

I'm George and [0]*those* people are my mother and my mother's sister. In this picture they're at a [1]______________. My mother's name is Rosanna and [2]______________ sister's name is Stefania. Mum and Aunt Stefania [3]______________ British. They're [4]______________ Italy. Aunt Stephania's purple [5]______________ and black shoes are fantastic!

[ ] / [5]

Writing

6 Answer the questions. Use the information below.

the USA

Mark

his T-shirt (black) and his hoodie (white)

his skateboard

11

0 Who is this?
1 Where is he from?
2 How old is he?
3 What are his favourite clothes?
4 What colour is his T-shirt?
5 What is his favourite thing?

This is Mark.

____
____
____
____
____

[ ] / [5]

Listening	[ ] / [10]	Communication	[ ] / [5]
Reading	[ ] / [10]	Writing	[ ] / [5]
		Your total score	[ ] / [30]

name ______________________ class ________

Listening

1 🔊 **2 Listen and write *T* (true) or *F* (false).**

0 Dan is Mateo's new neighbour. [T]
1 Mateo is from Spain. [ ]
2 Gabriella is eleven years old. [ ]
3 Peter is from the USA. [ ]
4 Anna's name isn't Chinese. [ ]
5 Anna's father is Polish. [ ]

[ ] / 5

2 🔊 **3 Listen and complete the sentences with one word.**

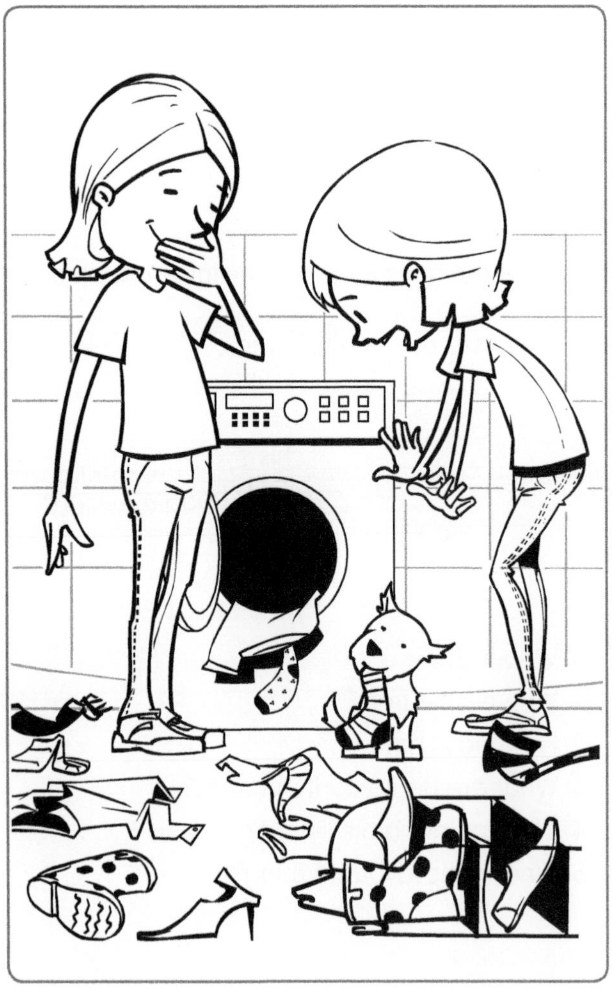

0 The boots are too *big*.
1 Granny's __________ is brown.
2 Mum's dress is __________ and white.
3 The red and purple __________ is cool.
4 The jeans are too __________.
5 The girl's __________ is orange.

[ ] / 5

Communication

3 Look at the pictures. Match sentences a–g with situations 1–5. There are two extra sentences.

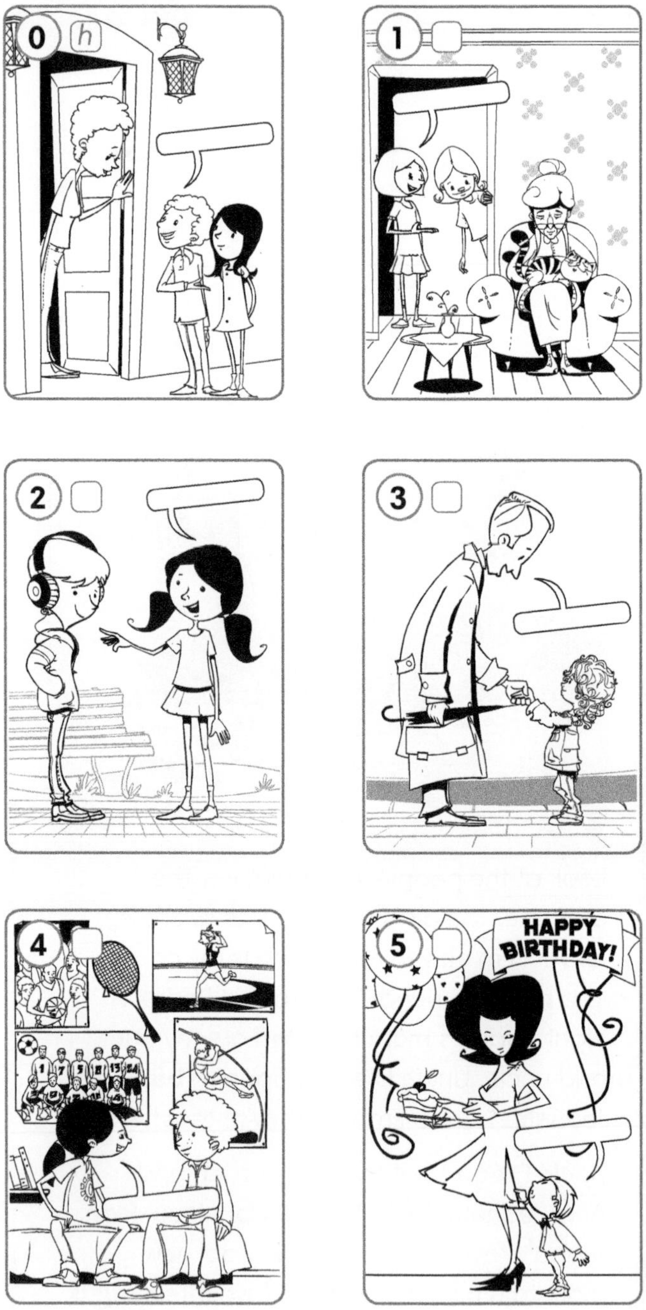

a What's 'kino' in English?
b She's my granny.
c How old are you?
d Who's your favourite sports person?
e Nice to meet you too.
f What's your favourite music?
g Where are you from?
h Mum, this is Nadia. She's my classmate.

[ ] / 5

name ______________________ class ________

Reading

4 Read the text. Then read the sentences and write *yes* or *no*.

HOME | ABOUT ME | CONTACT

Friday

My family pictures

by Miguel Sanchez

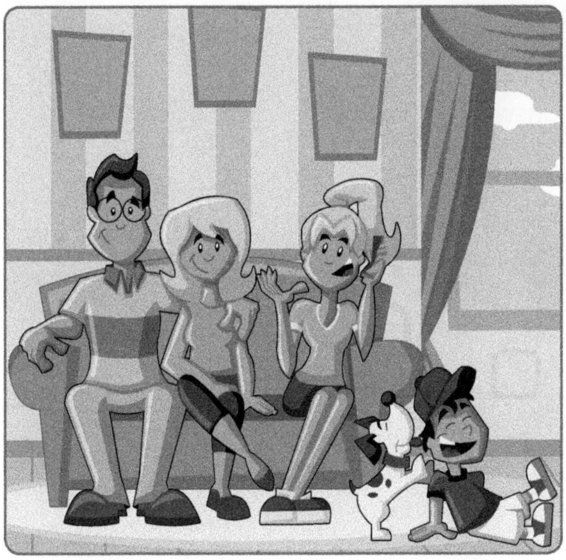

This is a picture of the Ricci family. They're at home. The girl's name is Roberta. She's eleven and I'm eleven too. Roberta is my cousin and my best friend. Her brother, Paolo, is seven. Roberta's mum and dad are my uncle and aunt. Uncle Antonio is from Italy but Aunt Madalene is French. They're actors. Uncle Antonio loves his new sports car and Aunt Madalene loves her pet dog, Bruno.

Paolo's favourite thing is his old skateboard and Roberta's hobby is playing the guitar. She's a great guitarist!

0 The people are at home. *yes*
1 Paolo's sister is seven years old. ______
2 Antonio is Italian. ______
3 Paolo's skateboard is new. ______
4 Madalene is Roberta's sister. ______
5 Bruno is Madalene's dog. ______

[ ] / 5

5 Complete the text with the words in the box. There is one extra word.

are	aren't	jacket	from	his	party	~~those~~

HOME | ABOUT ME | CONTACT

I'm Helen and [0]*those* people are my father and my father's sister. My father's name is Joe and [1]______ sister's name is Laura. Dad and Aunt Laura [2]______ British. They're [3]______ the USA. In this photo they're at a [4]______. Dad's black [5]______ is fantastic. And his trousers are cool too!

[ ] / 5

Writing

6 Answer the questions. Use the information below.

Biyu

China

her tracksuit (green) and her jeans (blue)

her mobile phone

12

0 Who is this?
1 Where is she from?
2 How old is she?
3 What are her favourite clothes?
4 What colour is her tracksuit?
5 What is her favourite thing?

This is Biyu.

____

____

____

____

____

[ ] / 5

Listening	[ ] / 10	Communication	[ ] / 5
Reading	[ ] / 10	Writing	[ ] / 5
		Your total score	[ ] / 30

name ______________________ class ______

Listening

1 🔊 4 Where are these things? Listen and draw lines.

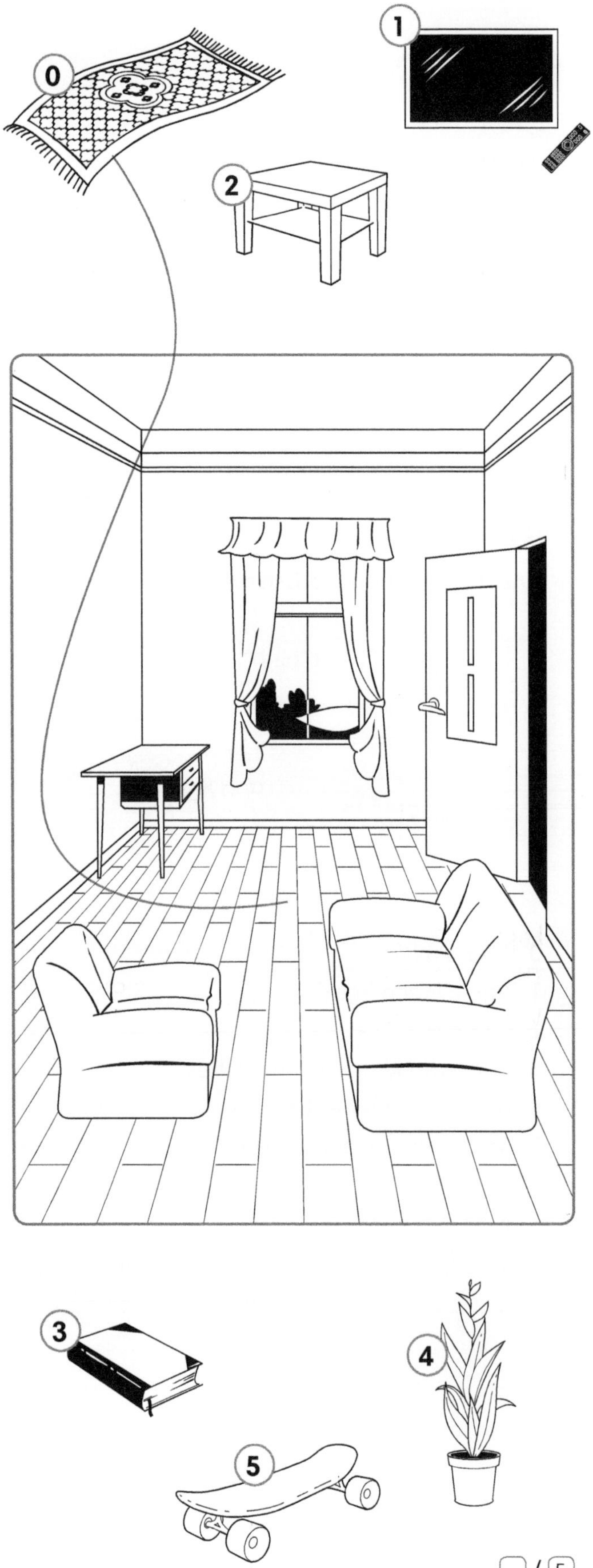

/5

2 🔊 5 Listen and complete the sentences with one word.

0 Darla is from Dublin, in *Ireland*.
1 She's got a __________ face.
2 Her hair is red and __________.
3 Darla gets good marks at school – she's __________.
4 Her dog's got big brown __________.
5 He's got a __________ little face.

/5

Communication

3 Read the dialogues and circle the correct answer.

0 A: Hello. Please come in.
B: a I'm fine thanks.
b Yes, all right.
c Thank you.

1 A: Would you like some cake?
B: a Yes, I am.
b No, thank you.
c I'm sorry.

2 A: Where's the bathroom, please?
B: a There's a bathroom.
b It's in the kitchen.
c It's upstairs.

3 A: Are there any trees in the garden?
B: a Yes, they are.
b No, it isn't.
c No, there aren't.

4 A: Where are my keys?
B: a I'm sorry. I've got them.
b That's all right.
c It's on the table.

5 A: Sorry, my mistake.
B: a No problem.
b Are you OK?
c Let me show you.

/5

3&4 Skills Test A

name ______________________ class ______

Reading

4 Read the text. Then read the sentences and write *T* (*true*) or *F* (*false*).

HOME | ABOUT ME | CONTACT

Our home

by Mary Jones

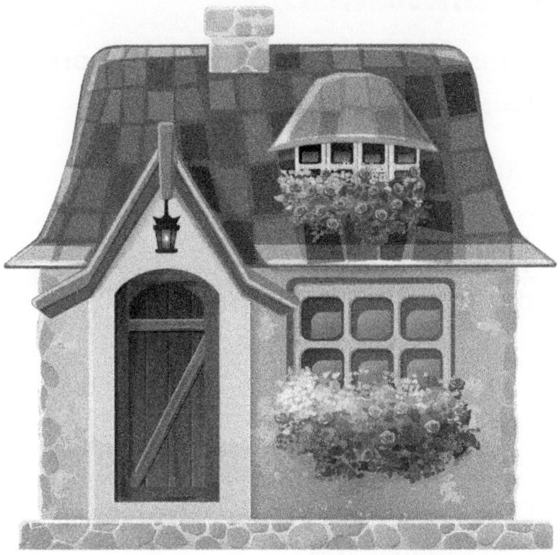

Our house is a small cottage in the country. The cottage is old, and old cottages haven't got big windows or many rooms. There's a living room, a bedroom for my parents, a bedroom for me and a bedroom for my sister. The bathroom is small but the kitchen is big. There are four chairs and a table in the kitchen. The table, chairs and the other things are old but the fridge is new.

We've got a car but there isn't a garage. Our garden is small but it's got fruit trees and flowers.

0 The house is a cottage. [*T*]
1 The windows of old cottages aren't big. [ ]
2 There are two bedrooms. [ ]
3 The bathroom and the kitchen are big. [ ]
4 The fridge isn't old. [ ]
5 There are some trees in the garden. [ ]

☐ / 5

5 Complete the text with the words in the box. There is one extra word.

~~are~~ dark door feet front has sofa

HOME | ABOUT ME | CONTACT

Rafael and Dominic are brothers. They [0]*are* very tall and they have got big [1]__________! Rafael [2]__________ got short [3]__________ hair but Dominic's hair is blond. Today they are at home, in the living room. Rafael is on the [4]__________ and Dominic is in [5]__________ of the window.

☐ / 5

Writing

6 Look at the information about your new friend. Then read the instructions and write about Veronica.

0 Name	Veronica
1 Personality	helpful
2 Eyes	big, green
3 Hair	long, straight, brown
4 Bedroom [✓]	a bed, a wardrobe, a desk, a chair
5 Bedroom [✗]	a carpet, a television

0 What is your new friend's name?
1 Write about her personality.
2 Write about her eyes.
3 Write about her hair.
4 Write about what there is in her bedroom.
5 Write about what there isn't in her bedroom.

My new friend's name is Veronica.

____

____

____

____

____

☐ / 5

Listening	☐ / 10	Communication	☐ / 5
Reading	☐ / 10	Writing	☐ / 5
		Your total score	☐ / 30

name ______________________ class ________

Listening

1 🔊 4 Where are these things? Listen and draw lines.

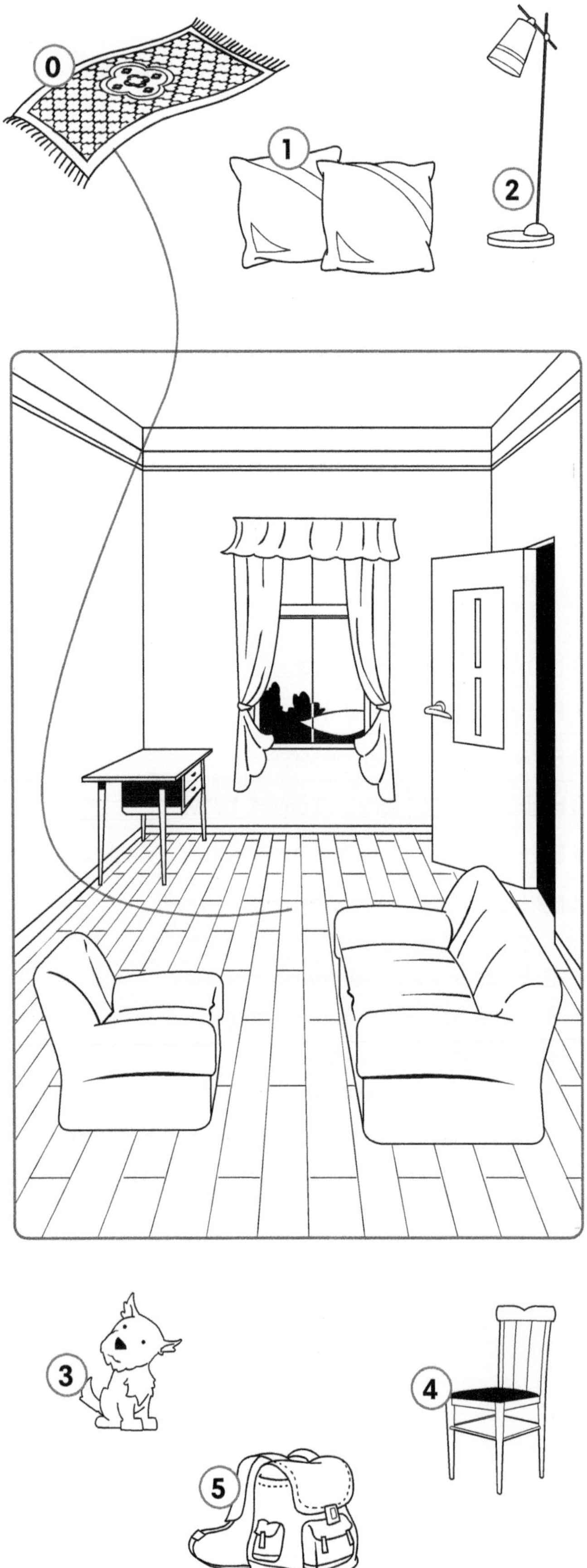

/ 5

2 🔊 5 Listen and complete the sentences with one word.

0 Darla is from Dublin, in *Ireland*.
1 Her ______________ are green.
2 She's got ______________ legs.
3 Darla is ______________ – she gets good marks at school.
4 Frisky's legs are ______________.
5 Frisky's little face is ______________.

/ 5

Communication

3 Read the dialogues and circle the correct answer.

0 **A:** Hello. Please come in.
B: **a** I'm fine thanks.
b Yes, all right.
[c] Thank you.

1 **A:** Is there a bike in the garage?
B: **a** Yes, it is.
b Yes, there is.
c No, there aren't.

2 **A:** Sorry about that!
B: **a** I'm fine.
b That's all right.
c Let me show you.

3 **A:** Would you like some water?
B: **a** Yes, please.
b No, I'm not.
c I'm sorry.

4 **A:** Where's the bathroom, please?
B: **a** It's downstairs.
b It's a bathroom.
c It's in the kitchen.

5 **A:** Where's my bag?
B: **a** That's all right.
b They're on the table.
c I'm sorry. I've got it.

/ 5

name _____   class _____

Reading

4 Read the text. Then read the sentences and write *T* (true) or *F* (false).

HOME | ABOUT ME | CONTACT

Our home
by Mary Jones

Our house is a small cottage in the country. The cottage is old, and old cottages haven't got big windows or many rooms. There's a living room, a bedroom for my parents, a bedroom for me and a bedroom for my sister. The bathroom is small but the kitchen is big. There are four chairs and a table in the kitchen. The table, chairs and the other things are old but the fridge is new.

We've got a car but there isn't a garage. Our garden is small but it's got fruit trees and flowers.

0	The house is a cottage.	T
1	Old cottages have got small windows.	
2	There are five rooms in the cottage.	
3	The kitchen and the bathroom are small.	
4	The car is in the garage.	
5	There are some flowers in the garden.	

◯ / 5

5 Complete the text with the words in the box. There is one extra word.

~~are~~ carpet dark door has next their

HOME | ABOUT ME | CONTACT

Samantha and Greta are sisters. They ⁰*are* short and ¹_____ hands and feet are small. Samantha ²_____ got long ³_____ hair but Greta's hair is short and blond. Today they are at home, in the living room. Samantha is on the ⁴_____ and Greta is ⁵_____ to the window.

◯ / 5

Writing

6 Look at the information about your new friend. Then read the instructions and write about Veronica.

0 Name	Veronica
1 Personality	helpful
2 Eyes	big, green
3 Hair	long, straight, brown
4 Bedroom [✓]	a bed, a wardrobe, a desk, a chair
5 Bedroom [✗]	a carpet, a television

0 What is your new friend's name?
1 Write about her personality.
2 Write about her eyes.
3 Write about her hair.
4 Write about what there is in her bedroom.
5 Write about what there isn't in her bedroom.

My new friend's name is Veronica.

_____
_____
_____
_____
_____

◯ / 5

Listening ◯ / 10	Communication ◯ / 5
Reading ◯ / 10	Writing ◯ / 5
	Your total score ◯ / 30

name _____ class _____

Listening

1 🔊 **6 Listen and tick the correct answer.**

0 What can Adam do?

 a ✓  b ☐  c ☐

1 Where is Sam's sister?

 a ☐  b ☐  c ☐

2 What can Mark play?

 a ☐  b ☐  c ☐

3 What club is on Wednesday?

 a ☐  b ☐  c ☐

4 What time is the football match on TV?

 a ☐  b ☐  c ☐

5 What does Ellen's dad do in the evening?

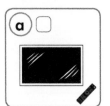 a ☐  b ☐  c ☐

☐ / 5

2 🔊 **7 Listen and write T (true) or F (false).**

0 Mum can't cook. `F`
1 Mum can fix cars and bikes. ☐
2 Dad cooks dinner at the weekend. ☐
3 Granny Sophie is my father's mother. ☐
4 Grandad Alex can play the guitar. ☐
5 Louis likes sport. ☐

☐ / 5

Communication

3 Complete the dialogues with the sentences in the box. There is one extra sentence.

> I agree.   It's at four o'clock.
> It's not a good idea.   It's quarter to seven.
> She can run fast.   The guitar.
> ~~Yes, let's do that!~~

0 A: Let's do something fun!
  B: *Yes, let's do that!*
1 A: What can your sister play?
  B: _____
2 A: What time is the match?
  B: _____
3 A: We can go ice-skating on Saturday.
  B: _____. I can't ice-skate.
4 A: Let's go swimming.
  B: _____. It's a hot day.
5 A: What time is it?
  B: _____

☐ / 5

name ____________ class ____

Reading

4 Read the text and write *yes* or *no*.

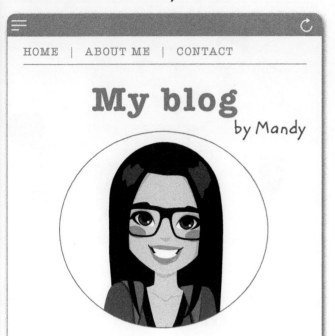

HOME | ABOUT ME | CONTACT

My blog

by Mandy

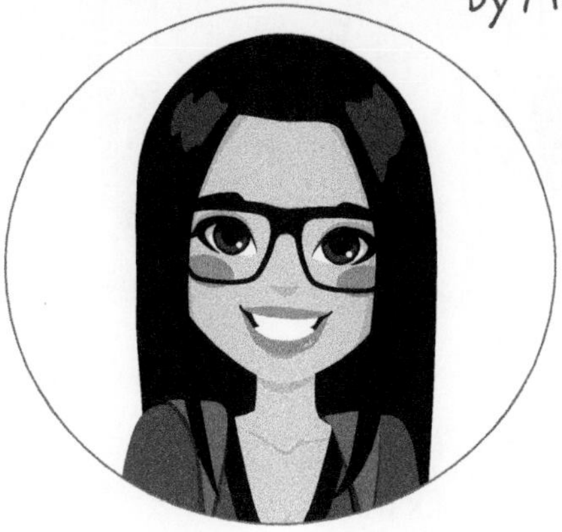

Hi! I'm Mandy and I'm twelve years old. I usually get up at seven o'clock and I have a shower. Then I have breakfast. I usually have orange juice and cornflakes, but sometimes I have milk, eggs and toast. I don't walk to school, I ride my bike.

I have lessons from half past eight to two o'clock. Then I go home and have lunch. I do my homework after lunch, but my best friend, Sarah, does her homework in the evening. On Mondays and Wednesdays, I play tennis in the afternoon. In the evening, I have dinner with my family. Then we watch TV. I go to bed at nine o'clock from Sunday to Thursday but on Fridays and Saturdays I go to bed at ten.

0 Mandy is twelve years old. *yes*
1 She always gets up at seven o'clock. ____
2 She always has milk, eggs and toast for breakfast. ____
3 She has lunch at home. ____
4 She sometimes plays tennis in the afternoon. ____
5 She goes to bed at nine o'clock on Fridays. ____

[ ] / [5]

5 Complete the text with the words in the box. There is one extra word.

August ~~June~~ listens often reads watches writes

HOME | ABOUT ME | CONTACT

My cousin Katie goes to school from September to 0 *June*, but in July and 1 ________ she is on holiday. She 2 ________ goes swimming in the morning. In the afternoon, she hangs out with her friends and in the evening she 3 ________ books and comics. She 4 ________ emails to her friends and 5 ________ to music.

[ ] / [5]

Writing

6 Write sentences about Fred's activities after school.

0	Mondays 3.00	do homework
1	Tuesdays 3.15	have a music lesson
2	Wednesdays 5.00	go to Art Club
3	Thursdays 4.30	play football with friends
4	Fridays 6.45	have dinner with family
5	Saturdays	hang out with friends, park

Fred does his homework at three o'clock on Mondays.

____
____
____
____
____
____
____
____
____
____

[ ] / [5]

Listening	[ ] / [10]	Communication	[ ] / [5]
Reading	[ ] / [10]	Writing	[ ] / [5]
		Your total score	[ ] / [30]

name _____   class _____

Listening

1 🔊 6 Listen and tick the correct answer.

0 What can Adam do?

 a ✓    b ☐    c ☐

1 Where is Sam's sister?

 a ☐    b ☐    c ☐

2 What can Mark play?

 a ☐    b ☐    c ☐

3 What club is on Wednesday?

 a ☐    b ☐    c ☐

4 What time is the football match on TV?

a ☐   b ☐   c ☐

5 What does Ellen's dad do in the evening?

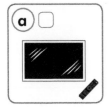 a ☐    b ☐    c ☐

☐ / 5

2 🔊 7 Listen and write *T* (true) or *F* (false).

0 Mum can't cook.   [F]
1 Mum can fix things.   ☐
2 Mum cooks breakfast at the weekend.   ☐
3 Granny Sophie can sing well.   ☐
4 Grandad Alex can draw well.   ☐
5 Louis goes to football matches
   on Sundays.   ☐

☐ / 5

Communication

3 **Complete the dialogues with the sentences in the box. There is one extra sentence.**

| Football.   He can act.   I agree. |
| I'm not sure.   It's at eight o'clock. |
| It's half past two.   ~~Yes, let's do that!~~ |

0 A: Let's do something fun!
   B: *Yes, let's do that!*

1 A: Let's go skateboarding this afternoon.
   B: _____. I can't skateboard.

2 A: What time is it?
   B: _____

3 A: We can go swimming this afternoon.
   B: _____. It's a hot day.

4 A: What can her brother do?
   B: _____

5 A: What time is the film?
   B: _____

☐ / 5

name   class

Reading

4 Read the text and write *yes* or *no*.

HOME | ABOUT ME | CONTACT

My blog
by Mandy

Hi! I'm Mandy and I'm twelve years old. I usually get up at seven o'clock and I have a shower. Then I have breakfast. I usually have orange juice and cornflakes, but sometimes I have milk, eggs and toast. I don't walk to school, I ride my bike.

I have lessons from half past eight to two o'clock. Then I go home and have lunch. I do my homework after lunch, but my best friend, Sarah, does her homework in the evening. On Mondays and Wednesdays, I play tennis in the afternoon. In the evening, I have dinner with my family. Then we watch TV. I go to bed at nine o'clock from Sunday to Thursday but on Fridays and Saturdays I go to bed at ten.

0 Mandy is twelve years old.   *yes*

1 She has breakfast and then she has a shower.   _____

2 She always has orange juice and cornflakes for breakfast.   _____

3 She goes home after school.   _____

4 Mandy's friend does her homework in the evening.   _____

5 Mandy goes to bed at ten o'clock on Tuesdays.   _____

⬜/ 5

5 Complete the text with the words in the box. There is one extra word.

July ~~June~~ listens reads usually watches writes

HOME | ABOUT ME | CONTACT

Josh goes to school from September to ⁰*June*, but in ¹_____ and August he is on holiday. In the morning, he hangs out with his friends. In the afternoon, he ²_____ goes swimming. In the evening, he ³_____ to music. He ⁴_____ comics and books and he sometimes ⁵_____ stories too.

⬜/ 5

Writing

6 Write sentences about Fred's activities after school.

0	Mondays 3.00	do homework
1	Tuesdays 3.15	have a music lesson
2	Wednesdays 5.00	go to Art Club
3	Thursdays 4.30	play football with friends
4	Fridays 6.45	have dinner with family
5	Saturdays	hang out with friends, park

Fred does his homework at three o'clock on Mondays.

_____
_____
_____
_____
_____
_____
_____
_____
_____
_____

⬜/ 5

Listening ⬜/ 10	Communication ⬜/ 5
Reading ⬜/ 10	Writing ⬜/ 5
	Your total score ⬜/ 30

name _____   class _____

Listening

1 🔊 8 Listen and match names 1–5 with pictures a–g. There are two extra pictures.

0 Martin	h	3 Irek	☐
1 Monique	☐	4 Cilla	☐
2 Tony	☐	5 Diana	☐

☐ / 5

2 🔊 9 Listen and write T (true) or F (false).

0 Sidney is a black dog. ☐ T
1 Sidney and Gertie go for a walk in the morning. ☐
2 There are rabbits in the park. ☐
3 Sidney likes the sea. ☐
4 Sidney and Gertie eat a lot of food. ☐
5 Sidney and Gertie like Ginger. ☐

☐ / 5

Communication

3 Complete the dialogues with the words and phrases in the box. There is one extra word.

> ~~help~~ here are please snowy who whose you are

A: Can I ⁰*help* you?

B: Can I have two tickets to the museum, ¹_____?

A: That's ten pounds.

B: Here ²_____.

A: And ³_____ your tickets.

B: Thanks.

A: What's the weather like in winter in Poland?

B: It's usually cold and ⁴_____.

A: ⁵_____ pet is that dog?

B: It's Lily's.

☐ / 5

&8 Skills Test A

_______________________________ name   ________ class

Reading

4 Read the text and answer the questions with a word or a number.

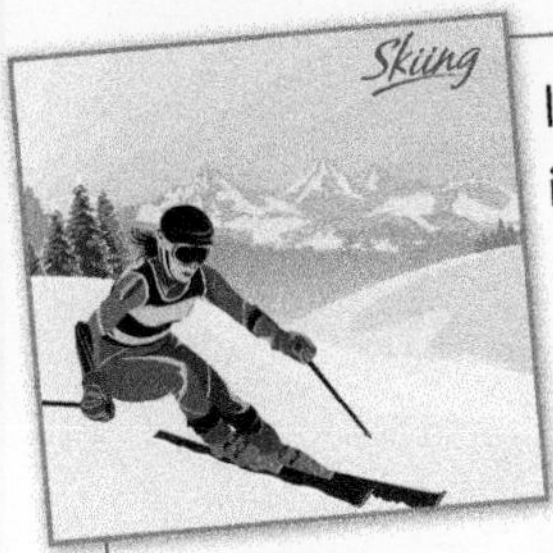

I'm from Tasmania, in Australia. In the summer we go to the beach every day. My favourite summer sport is windsurfing. I like swimming and sailing too. It's too cold for water sports in the winter. In July and August it's snowy but I don't mind. Then my mum and I go skiing in the mountains. My father doesn't like skiing. He thinks it's dangerous.

Anneli, 11

I'm from Botswana, in Africa. I'm not sporty but I love horse-riding and the best place for horse-riding is Botswana. You can go riding all year. From January to April it's warm at night and hot in the day. In May it's cool at night but days are warm. In June, July and August the weather is cold at night but warm in the day. You can ride for hours and you can see lions, giraffes, elephants, antelopes and zebras. It's cool!

Bruce, 13

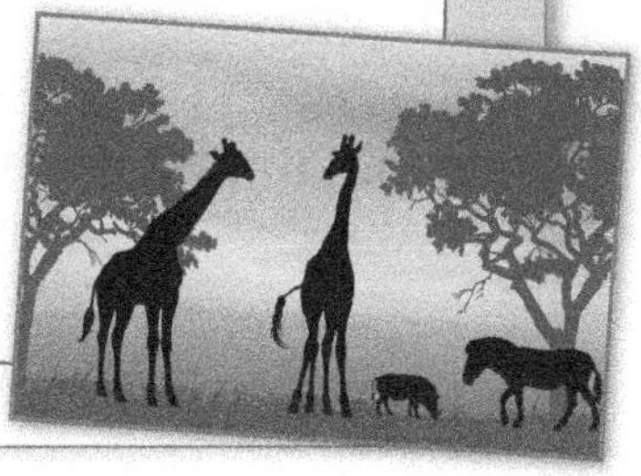

0 What nationality is Anneli?
Australian.

1 What is her favourite summer sport?
____

2 What sport does she do in the winter?
____

3 Why doesn't her father like skiing?
He thinks it is __________________.

4 What is the weather like in Botswana in January in the day?
It is __________________.

5 How many different animals can you see?
____

☐ / [5]

5 Complete the text with the words in the box. There is one extra word.

brushes ~~does~~ doesn't going it them vegetables

Marina [0] *does* a lot of exercise and she likes [1] __________ to bed early. What else does she do to keep healthy? She [2] __________ her teeth after every meal. She eats lots of fruit and [3] __________. She loves [4] __________. But she [5] __________ drink a lot of water.

☐ / [5]

Writing

6 Look at the fact file about Penny's pet. Then use the information and write about her pet.

Pet:	a rat 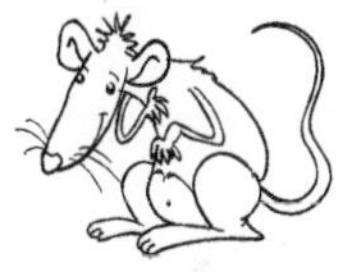
Colour:	white and brown
Food:	vegetables, dog food
Abilities:	can do tricks
Personality:	clever, playful
Likes:	playing with people, sleeping

Penny's pet is a rat.

____

____

____

____

____

____

____

____

☐ / [5]

Listening	☐ / [10]	Communication	☐ / [5]
Reading	☐ / [10]	Writing	☐ / [5]
		Your total score	☐ / [30]

name ______________________ class ________

Listening

1 8 Listen and match names 1–5 with pictures a–g. There are two extra pictures.

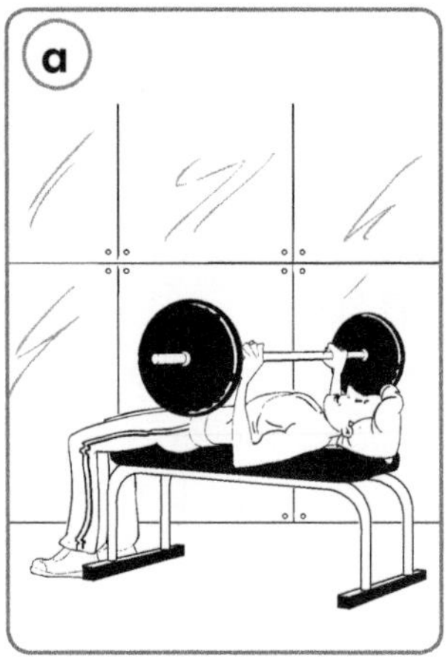

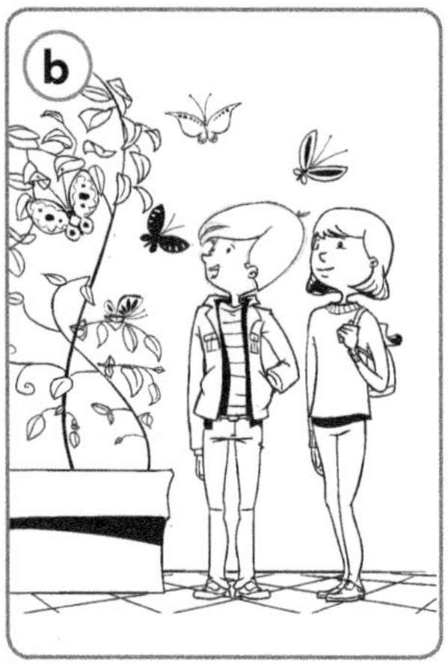

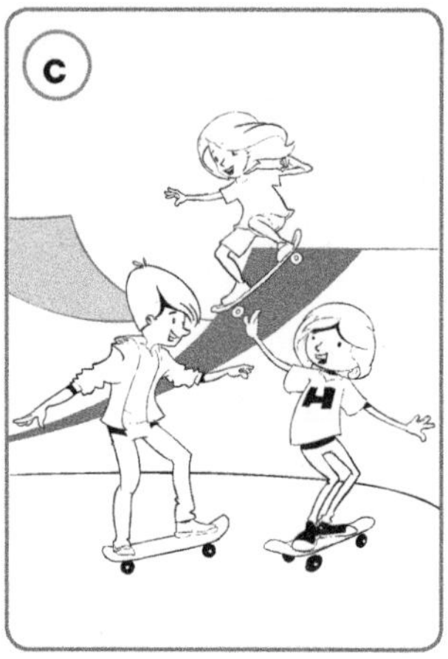

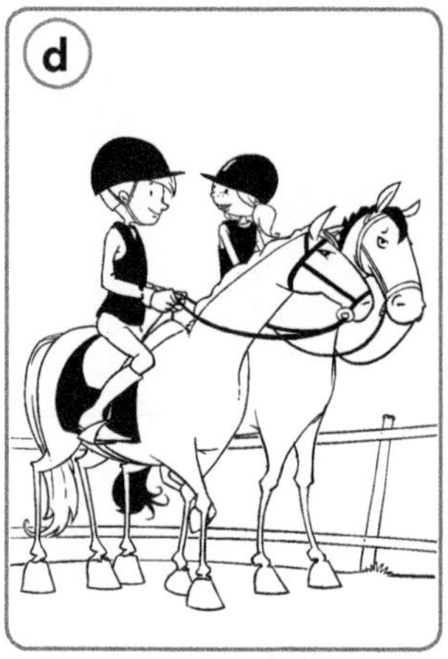

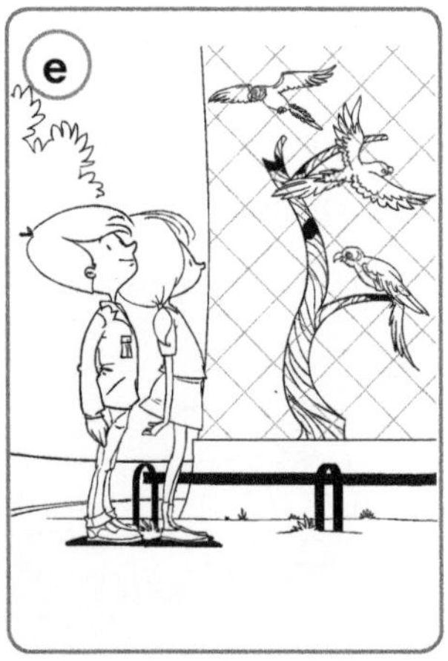

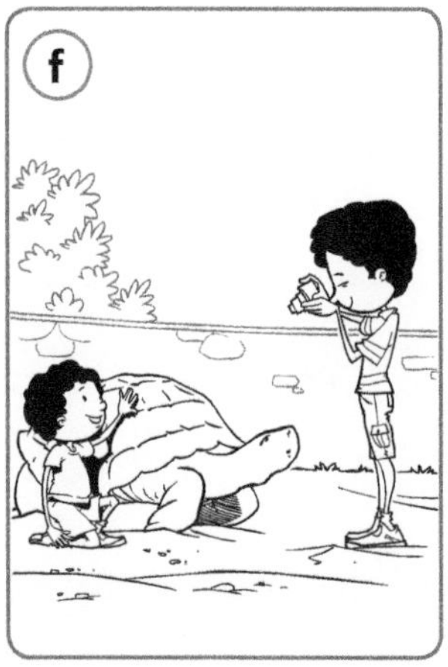

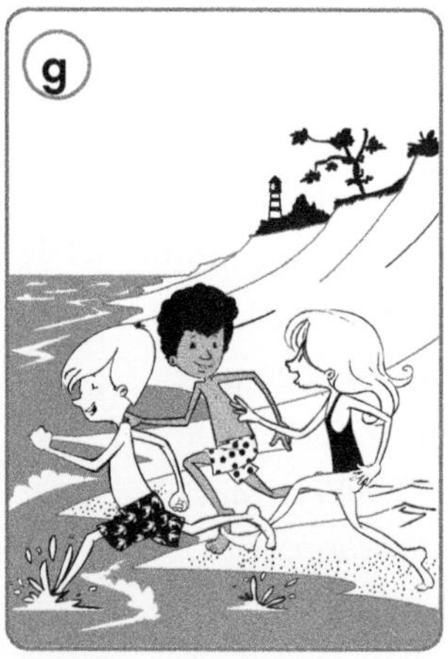

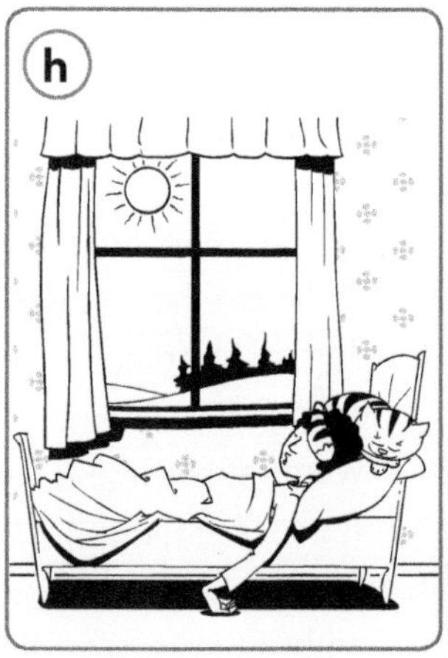

0 Martin [*h*]
1 Monique [ ]
2 Tony [ ]
3 Irek [ ]
4 Cilla [ ]
5 Diana [ ]

[ ] / [5]

2 9 Listen and write *T* (true) or *F* (false).

0 Gertie is a cute dog. [*T*]
1 Sidney and Gertie go for a walk after dinner. [ ]
2 Gertie likes swimming. [ ]
3 Gertie doesn't eat a lot of food. [ ]
4 There are three pets in the house. [ ]
5 Ginger loves the dogs. [ ]

[ ] / [5]

Communication

3 Complete the dialogues with the words and phrases in the box. There is one extra word.

have ~~help~~ like that's when where you are

A: Can I [0]*help* you?
B: Can I [1] ______________ one ticket to the museum, please?
A: [2] ______________ four pounds fifty.
B: Here [3] ______________.
A: And here's your ticket.
B: Thanks.

A: What's the weather [4] ______________ in summer in Australia?
B: It's usually hot and sunny.
A: [5] ______________ do you usually go on holiday?
B: To Spain.

[ ] / [5]

name ______________________ class ________

Reading

4 Read the text and answer the questions with a word or a number.

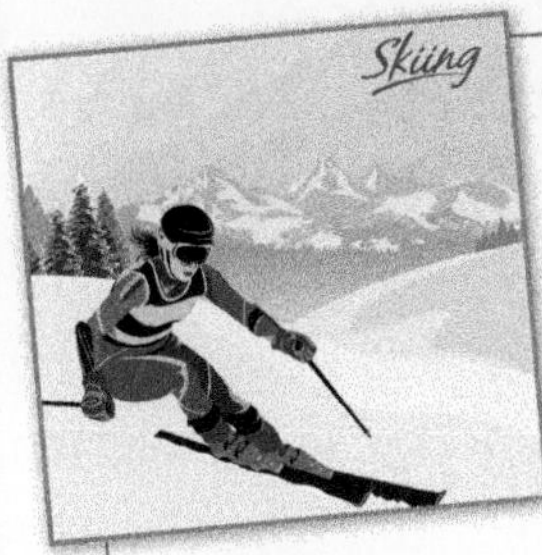

I'm from Tasmania, in Australia. In the summer we go to the beach every day. My favourite summer sport is windsurfing. I like swimming and sailing too. It's too cold for water sports in the winter. In July and August it's snowy but I don't mind. Then my mum and I go skiing in the mountains. My father doesn't like skiing. He thinks it's dangerous.

Anneli, 11

I'm from Botswana, in Africa. I'm not sporty but I love horse-riding and the best place for horse-riding is Botswana. You can go riding all year. From January to April it's warm at night and hot in the day. In May it's cool at night but days are warm. In June, July and August the weather is cold at night but warm in the day. You can ride for hours and you can see lions, giraffes, elephants, antelopes and zebras. It's cool!

Bruce, 13

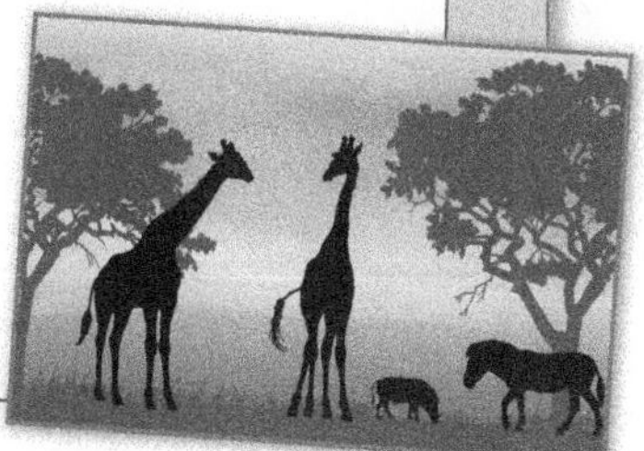

0 What nationality is Anneli?
Australian.
1 Where does she always go in the summer?
To the ______________________
2 What other water sports does she do?
Windsurfing, swimming and ______________
3 Where does she go skiing?
In the ______________________
4 What activity does Bruce love?
____
5 What's the weather like in Botswana in July at night?
It is ______________________.

☐ / 5

5 Complete the text with the words in the box. There is one extra word.

brushes do does drinks eating ~~goes~~ them

Mike usually [0] *goes* to bed early because he wants to be healthy. He [1] __________ his teeth after every meal. He likes [2] __________ sweets but he doesn't eat lots of [3] __________. He [4] __________ a lot of water and he [5] __________ a lot of exercise too.

☐ / 5

Writing

6 Look at the fact file about Penny's pet. Then use the information and write about her pet.

Pet:	a rat 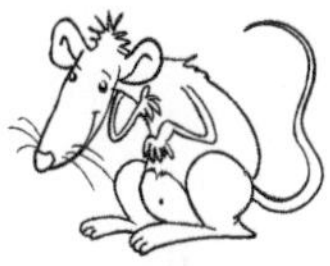
Colour:	white and brown
Food:	vegetables, dog food
Abilities:	can do tricks
Personality:	clever, playful
Likes:	playing with people, sleeping

Penny's pet is a rat.
____
____
____
____
____
____
____
____

☐ / 5

Listening	☐ / 10	Communication	☐ / 5
Reading	☐ / 10	Writing	☐ / 5
		Your total score	☐ / 30

Mid-Year Test A

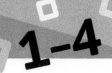

name ______________________ class ________

Vocabulary

1 Circle the correct word.

Jean isn't ⁰*Britain* / *British*. He's from ¹*France* / *French*. He's got short, ²*spiky* / *dark*, blond hair and big, brown ³*ears* / *eyes*. He's a nice boy and he's ⁴*boring* / *clever* too. He gets good marks ⁵*at* / *on* school.

☐ / 5

2 Look at the picture and complete the text with the words in the box. There is one extra word.

console ~~home~~ in front of kitchen living mobile window

My family and I are at ⁰home today. Dad is in the ¹__________ and Mum and I are in the ²__________ room. There's a games ³__________ on the table and there's a television ⁴__________ the sofa. There's a plant next to the ⁵__________.

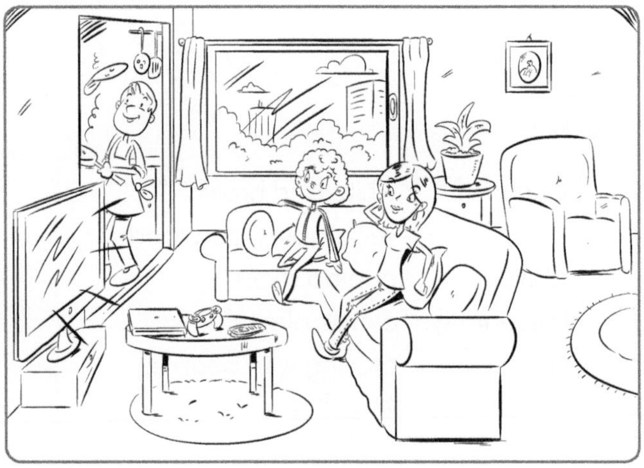

☐ / 5

3 Circle the correct answer.

0 *Purple* / *Oranges* / *Rubber* is my favourite colour.
1 The baby has got ten pink *teeth* / *foot* / *toes*.
2 Her blue *jeans* / *tracksuit* / *trousers* is too small for her.
3 My aunt's daughter is my *cousin* / *uncle* / *sister*.
4 These clothes aren't boring. They're *cool* / *long* / *short*!
5 The *hoodies* / *caps* / *shoes* are on my feet.

☐ / 5

Grammar

4 Match beginnings 1–5 with endings a–e.

0 Is there	f	a any armchairs in the living room?
1 Are there	☐	b the students in the park?
2 Are	☐	c your T-shirts?
3 Have	☐	d you got a brother?
4 What	☐	e has she got?
5 Are those	☐	f a fridge in the kitchen?

☐ / 5

5 Circle the correct answer.

HOME | ABOUT ME | CONTACT

We ⁰____ got a house in the country. There aren't ¹____ houses next to our house. There ²____ a garage but there is a small garden with ³____ apple tree. The house ⁴____ got three bedrooms. ⁵____ is my bedroom. It is my favourite room.

0	**a** have	**b** has	**c** are
1	**a** a	**b** an	**c** any
2	**a** is	**b** isn't	**c** are
3	**a** a	**b** an	**c** any
4	**a** is	**b** have	**c** has
5	**a** This	**b** These	**c** Those

☐ / 5

6 Complete the sentences. Use one word in each gap.

0 Are you twelve years old, Diana?
1 I've got a pet dog. I__________ name is Mutt.
2 Clara has got blue eyes. H__________ hair is brown.
3 Kate and Joe have got two children. T__________ names are Charles and Alfie.
4 Are Mum and Dad in the garden? Yes, t__________ are.
5 My sister and I aren't in the park. W__________ are at home.

☐ / 5

Vocabulary	☐ / 15	Grammar	☐ / 15
		Your total score	☐ / 30

name _____   class _____

Listening

7 🔊 **10** Listen and complete the table. Write a number or a word.

Name	Hair	Age
Jack	short, ⁰<u>black</u>	¹ _____
Tom	² _____, spiky	³ _____
Jenny	⁴ _____, wavy, ⁵ _____	6 _____

☐ / ⑥

Communication

8 Complete the dialogues with the sentences and questions in the box.

> Can you help me, please?   Hello, Kevin. Nice to meet you.   ~~How do you spell 'sharpener'?~~
> Sorry, my mistake.   What's 'lustro' in English?
> Where are you from?   Where's the bathroom, please?   Who's your favourite actor?
> Would you like a sweet?

0 A: *How do you spell 'sharpener'?*
   B: S-H-A-R-P-E-N-E-R.

1 A: _____
   B: Mirror.

2 A: _____
   B: Nice to meet you too.

3 A: _____
   B: Madrid, in Spain.

4 A: _____
   B: It's upstairs.

5 A: _____
   B: No problem.

6 A: _____
   B: Yes, of course.

7 A: _____
   B: No, thank you.

8 A: _____
   B: Ryan Gosling.

☐ / ⑧

Reading

9 Read the text and answer the questions. Write full sentences.

HOME | ABOUT ME | CONTACT

My grandparents aren't in the UK. They're in Italy. Their house is next to the sea. Granny has got a garden. It's in front of the house. Grandad has got an old car and a new car. They're in the garage next to the house.

The house is perfect for holidays. It's got one bedroom for my grandparents, one for my parents and one for me! There's a small bathroom too. The kitchen is the only big room. It's got a fridge, a table, some chairs and an old sofa. And it's got a television! It's fantastic!

Rosanna, 11

0 Where are Rosanna's grandparents?
   They're in Italy.

1 What is in front of the house?
   _____

2 Where is the garage?
   _____

3 Has Rosanna's grandad got two cars?
   _____

4 How many bedrooms are there in the house?
   _____

5 Is the bathroom big?
   _____

6 Where is the television?
   _____

☐ / ⑥

| Listening | ☐ / ⑥ | Communication | ☐ / ⑧ |
| Reading | ☐ / ⑥ | **Your total score** | ☐ / ⑳ |

1–4 Mid-Year Test B

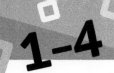

name ______________________ class ______

Vocabulary

1 Circle the correct word.

Teresa isn't ⁰*Britain* / *British*. She's from ¹*Poland* / *Polish*. She's got long, ²*wavy* / *blond* dark hair and big, blue ³*ears* / *eyes*. She's a nice girl. She's ⁴*boring* / *funny* too, and she tells great jokes. Teresa is in my class ⁵*on* / *at* school.

/5

2 Look at the picture and complete the text with the words in the box. There is one extra word.

~~home~~	in front of	kitchen	living	mobile
on	plant			

My family and I are at ⁰home today. Mum and I are in the ¹______________ room. There's a ²______________ phone on the table and there's a sofa ³______________ the television. There's a ⁴______________ next to the window. Dad is in the ⁵______________.

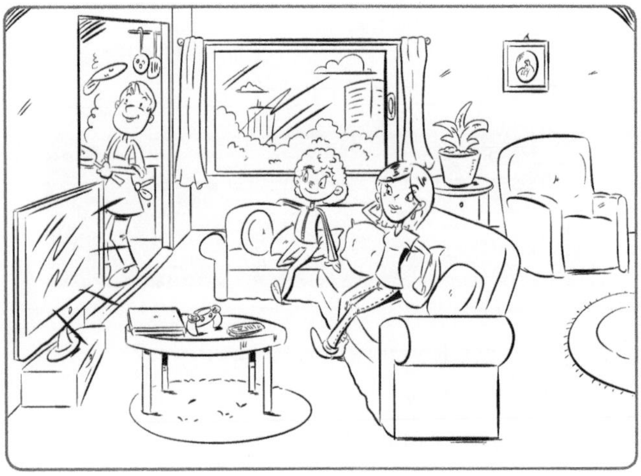

/5

3 Circle the correct answer.

0 *Purple* / *Oranges* / *Rubber* is my favourite colour.
1 My uncle's son is my *brother* / *father* / *cousin*.
2 The baby has got ten pink *tooth* / *toes* / *feet*.
3 His red *trainers* / *hoodie* / *jeans* is too small for him.
4 The *boots* / *tracksuits* / *caps* are on my feet.
5 That shirt isn't cool. It's *boring* / *grey* / *new*!

/5

Grammar

4 Match beginnings 1–5 with endings a–e.

0 Have [f]
1 Is there [ ]
2 Are there [ ]
3 What [ ]
4 Are these [ ]
5 Are [ ]

a a bath in the bathroom?
b your friends in the classroom?
c has he got?
d Anna's clothes?
e any trees in the garden?
f they got grandparents?

/5

5 Circle the correct answer.

HOME | ABOUT ME | CONTACT

Mr and Mrs Johnson ⁰____ got a house in the country. There is a small garden with ¹____ orange tree, but there aren't ²____ flowers. There ³____ a garage. The house ⁴____ got four bedrooms. ⁵____ is my bedroom. It's my favourite room.

0	**a** have	**b** has	**c** are
1	**a** any	**b** a	**c** an
2	**a** an	**b** any	**c** a
3	**a** isn't	**b** aren't	**c** haven't
4	**a** is	**b** has	**c** have
5	**a** These	**b** Those	**c** That

/5

6 Complete the sentences. Use one word in each gap.

0 Are you twelve years old, Diana?
1 Gerry has got a pet cat. I__________ name is Taffy.
2 You and Gloria have got brown eyes. Y__________ hair is brown too.
3 My friend and I are in the park. W__________ aren't at school.
4 Are Barbara and Sam in the garden? No, t__________ aren't.
5 Sarah and Bill have got two children. T__________ names are Paul and Amy.

/5

Vocabulary	/15	Grammar	/15
		Your total score	/30

name _____   class _____

Listening

7 🔊 **10** Listen and complete the table. Write a number or a word.

Name	Hair	Age
Jack	short, ⁰black	¹ _____
Tom	dark, ² _____	³ _____
Jenny	long, ⁴ _____, ⁵ _____	⁶ _____

◯ / 6

Communication

8 Complete the dialogues with the sentences and questions in the box.

> Can you help me?   Hello, Adam. Nice to meet you.   ~~How do you spell 'sharpener'?~~
> Sorry about that!   What's 'ołówek' in English?
> What's your favourite film?   Where's my coat?
> Where is she from?   Where's the bathroom, please?

0 A: *How do you spell 'sharpener'?*
  B: S-H-A-R-P-E-N-E-R.

1 A: _____
  B: Nice to meet you too.

2 A: _____
  B: That's all right.

3 A: _____
  B: Pencil.

4 A: _____
  B: Yes, of course.

5 A: _____
  B: Bristol, in the UK.

6 A: _____
  B: Let me show you.

7 A: _____
  B: Over there.

8: A: _____
  B: *The Lion King.*

◯ / 8

Reading

9 Read the text and answer the questions. Write full sentences.

HOME | ABOUT ME | CONTACT

My aunt and uncle aren't in the UK. They're in Spain. Their house is next to the sea. Aunt Dolores has got a garden. It's in front of the house. Uncle Miguel has got an old car and a new car. They're in the garage next to the house.

The house is perfect for holidays. It's got one bedroom for my aunt and uncle, one for my parents and one for me! There's a small bathroom too. The kitchen is the only big room. It's got a fridge, a table, some chairs and an old armchair. And it's got a television! It's fantastic!

Juan, 11

0 Where are Juan's aunt and uncle?
  They're in Spain.

1 Where is the house?
  _____

2 What is next to the house?
  _____

3 Has Juan's uncle got two cars?
  _____

4 How many bedrooms are there in the house?
  _____

5 How many big rooms are there in the house?
  _____

6 Where is the armchair?
  _____

◯ / 6

| Listening ◯ / 6 | Communication ◯ / 8 |
| Reading ◯ / 6 | **Your total score** ◯ / 20 |

1–8 End-of-Year Test A

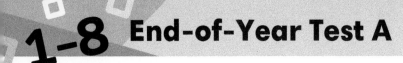

name ______________________ class ________

Vocabulary

1 Circle the odd one out.

0	orange	green	grey	lemon
1	bird	snake	butterfly	parrot
2	Monday	May	June	July
3	badminton	tennis	sailing	volleyball
4	bedroom	garden	kitchen	living room
5	neck	arms	hands	fingers

☐ / 5

2 Complete the text. Circle the correct answer.

HOME | ABOUT ME | CONTACT

My best friend's name is Donna Marks. She's from [0]*USA* / *the USA* but she lives in London. She's friendly and everyone likes her. Donna is [1]*slow* / *sporty*. She plays basketball and she [2]*goes* / *does* taekwondo. She likes watching films and she's got lots of film posters on the [3]*walls* / *floors* in her bedroom. Donna has got a pet [4]*rabbit* / *whale*. His name is Bugs and he's got long ears and a pink nose. Bugs is cute and he's [5]*wavy* / *fast* too.

☐ / 5

3 Complete the email with the words in the box. There is one extra word.

drink early football guitar ~~home~~ on out

Hi Jamie!

How are you? I'm not at [0]*home*. I'm [1]__________ holiday with Mum and Dad in Italy. My Mum's family live in Sicily. Here, we don't go to bed [2]__________. It's too hot! We go swimming in the sea every day and we [3]__________ a lot of water. We eat a lot of fruit and vegetables too. In the evening, we hang [4]__________ with all the family. Uncle Enzo and Aunt Susanna play the [5]__________ and we sing old Italian songs. It's great!

Lucia

☐ / 5

Grammar

4 Circle the correct word.

0 I'm Ann and *me* / *my* / *you* brother's name is Tim.
1 My family and I are Chinese but *your* / *our* / *us* home is in Canada.
2 Spiders are ugly and I hate *they* / *it* / *them*!
3 This cat is brown but *that* / *those* cats are white.
4 *Ewa* / *Ewa's* eyes are blue, not brown.
5 Are there *a* / *any* lions in India?

☐ / 5

5 Use the correct form of the verbs in the text.

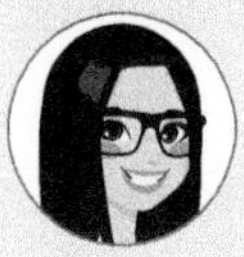

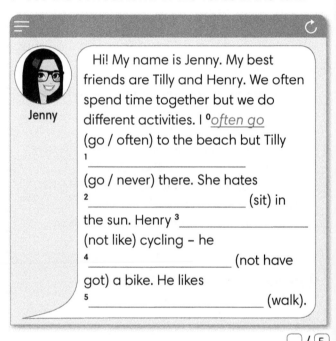

Jenny

Hi! My name is Jenny. My best friends are Tilly and Henry. We often spend time together but we do different activities. I [0]*often go* (go / often) to the beach but Tilly [1]__________________ (go / never) there. She hates [2]__________________ (sit) in the sun. Henry [3]__________________ (not like) cycling – he [4]__________________ (not have got) a bike. He likes [5]__________________ (walk).

☐ / 5

6 Write the questions.

0 **A:** Have *you got* a new car?
B: No, we haven't got a new car.
1 **A:** __________ a rat under the table?
B: Yes, there is a rat under the table!
2 **A:** ________ your mum ________ for the family?
B: No, my mum doesn't cook for the family, but my dad cooks well.
3 **A:** Where __________________ live?
B: Her grandparents live in Warsaw.
4 **A:** Whose __________________ it?
B: It's Mike's mountain bike.
5 **A:** __________________ golf?
B: No, I can't play golf. I don't like sports.

☐ / 5

Vocabulary	☐ / 15	Grammar	☐ / 15
		Your total score	☐ / 30

name _____ class _____

Listening

7 🔊 11 **Read the questions. Then listen and complete the notes about Henry and Rosie. Use one, two or three words.**

Henry

0 Does Henry like getting up early? *Yes, he does.*

1 What time does Henry get up?
At _____ o'clock.

2 Is he sporty? _____

3 What sports does he play?
Football and _____

Rosie

4 Does Rosie hate getting up early? _____

5 What can she draw? _____

6 What can't she do? She _____

☐ / 6

Communication

8 **Circle the correct answer.**

0 A: (What's) / Who's your favourite sport?
B: Windsurfing.

1 A: Hello. Please *walk / come* in.
B: Thank you.

2 A: Erin, *it / this* is my aunt.
B: Hello, Erin.

3 A: Nice to meet you.
B: Nice to meet you *too / please*.

4 A: Where's the bathroom, please?
B: *Let / Like* me show you.

5 A: Sorry *at / about* that!
B: That's all right.

6 A: *Do / Would* you like a sandwich?
B: No, thank you.

7 A: *Can / Let's* go rock climbing!
B: I'm not sure.

8 A: What's the weather *likes / like*?
B: It's warm.

☐ / 8

Reading

9 **Read the blog. Then read the sentences and write *T* (true), *F* (false) or *DS* (doesn't say).**

HOME | ABOUT ME | CONTACT

My favourite animals

My favourite animals are spider monkeys. They've got a small head, long arms and long legs. Their hair is black or brown. They've got four long fingers on their hands, but there are five toes on their feet. They've also got a long tail.

They live in trees in Brazil and Mexico and they can jump from tree to tree. They're fast! They play in the trees and sleep there too. They sometimes come down from the trees and walk on the ground. There are usually thirty spider monkeys in a family.

Spider monkeys are clever. They're cute too, and I love them.

What are your favourite animals?

0 Spider monkeys have got a long head. ☐ F

1 Spider monkeys have got black or brown hair. ☐

2 Spider monkeys haven't got five fingers on their hands. ☐

3 They live and sleep in trees. ☐

4 They never walk on the ground. ☐

5 They can't swim. ☐

6 They have got small families. ☐

☐ / 6

| Listening ☐ / 6 | Communication ☐ / 8 |
| Reading ☐ / 6 | **Your total score** ☐ / 20 |

name _____   class _____

Vocabulary

1 Circle the odd one out.

0	orange	green	grey	(lemon)
1	tortoise	bird	parrot	butterfly
2	August	May	April	Friday
3	tennis	football	basketball	badminton
4	bathroom	living room	garden	kitchen
5	legs	feet	toes	head

◯ / 5

2 Complete the text. Circle the correct answer.

HOME | ABOUT ME | CONTACT

My best friend's name is Angela Standley. She's from ⁰USA / (the USA) but she lives in London. She's nice and everyone likes her. Angela is ¹slow / sporty. She ²goes / does taekwondo and she plays volleyball. She loves reading comics and she's got a great poster of Batman on the ³door / floor in her bedroom. Angela has got a pet ⁴goldfish / hamster. His name is Phil. He's small and round, with small ears. Phil is cute and he's ⁵fast / wavy too!

◯ / 5

3 Complete the email with the words in the box. There is one extra word.

early   eat   football   guitar   hang   ~~home~~   on

Hi Lily!

How are you? I'm not at ⁰_home_. I'm in Italy with Mum and Dad. We're ¹_____ holiday. My aunts, uncles and cousins live in Sicily. It's hot here in summer and we don't go to bed ²_____. We go swimming in the sea every day. We ³_____ fruit and vegetables and drink a lot of water. In the evening, we ⁴_____ out with all the family. Aunt Lucilla and Uncle Dario play the ⁵_____ and we sing old Italian songs. It's great!

Lucia

◯ / 5

Grammar

4 Circle the correct word.

0 I'm Ann and me / (my) / you brother's name is Tim.
1 Those dogs have got long legs but these / this dog has got short legs.
2 Puppies are cute and I love they / it / them!
3 My family and I are Spanish but your / our / us home is in Britain.
4 Is there a / any tiger in the zoo?
5 Joe / Joe's brother is 17 years old, not 15.

◯ / 5

5 Use the correct form of the verbs in the text.

Jenny

Hi! My name is Jenny. My best friends are Jill and Steve. We often spend time together but we do different activities. I ⁰_never go_ (go / never) to the sea but Jill ¹_____ (go / always) there. She loves ²_____ (sit) in the sun. Steve ³_____ (not like) skateboarding – he ⁴_____ (not have got) a skateboard. He likes ⁵_____ (run).

◯ / 5

6 Write the questions.

0 A: Have _you got_ a new car?
  B: No, we haven't got a new car.
1 A: _____ your dad _____ for the family?
  B: No, my dad doesn't cook for the family, but my mum cooks well.
2 A: Whose _____ it?
  B: It's Clara's games console.
3 A: _____ hockey?
  B: Yes, I can play hockey. I love sports.
4 A: Where _____ live?
  B: Their cousins live in Hong Kong.
5 A: _____ a skateboard in the wardrobe?
  B: No, there isn't a skateboard in the wardrobe!

◯ / 5

Vocabulary ◯ / 15   Grammar ◯ / 15
Your total score ◯ / 30

name _____   class _____

Listening

7 🔊 11 Read the questions. Then listen and complete the notes about Henry and Rosie. Use one, two or three words.

Henry

0 Does Henry like getting up early? *Yes, he does.*

1 What time does Henry have breakfast?
At _____

2 Where does he ride his bike? To _____

3 Can he run fast? _____

Rosie

4 Is Rosie often late for school?
_____

5 What can she write? She can _____

6 What does she want to be?
An _____

☐ / ⑥

Communication

8 Circle the correct answer.

0 A: (What's) / Who's your favourite sport?
B: Windsurfing.

1 A: *Do / Would* you like a cupcake?
B: Yes, please.

2 A: Nice to meet you.
B: Nice to meet you *too / there*.

3 A: Hello. Please *walk / come* in.
B: Thank you.

5 A: Sorry *about / at* that!
B: That's all right.

5 A: Liam, *this / he* is my uncle.
B: Hello, Liam.

6 A: Where's the bathroom, please?
B: Let me *see / show* you.

7 A: *When / Where* can we go roller skating?
B: On Friday.

8 A: *What's / Where's* the weather like?
B: It's cold and cloudy.

☐ / ⑧

Reading

9 Read the blog. Then read the sentences and write *T* (true), *F* (false) or *DS* (doesn't say).

HOME | ABOUT ME | CONTACT

My favourite animals

My favourite animals are spider monkeys. They've got a small head, long arms and long legs. Their hair is black or brown. They've got four long fingers on their hands, but there are five toes on their feet. They've also got a long tail.

They live in trees in Brazil and Mexico and they can jump from tree to tree. They're fast! They play in the trees and sleep there too. They sometimes come down from the trees and walk on the ground. There are usually thirty spider monkeys in a family.

Spider monkeys are clever. They're cute too, and I love them.

What are your favourite animals?

0 Spider monkeys have got a long head. ☐ F

1 Their arms and legs are long. ☐

2 Spider monkeys have got five fingers on their hands. ☐

3 They have got five toes on their feet. ☐

4 They can swim. ☐

5 They sometimes walk on the ground. ☐

6 There are usually thirteen spider monkeys in a family. ☐

☐ / ⑥

| Listening ☐ / ⑥ | Communication ☐ / ⑧ |
| Reading ☐ / ⑥ | **Your total score** ☐ / ⑳ |

name _____ class _____

Part 1 Reading and Writing

Look and read. Put a tick [✓] or a cross [✗] in the box. There are two examples.

Examples

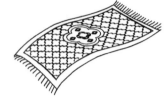

0 These are shoes. ✓   **0** This is a floor. ✗

Questions

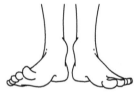

1 These are teeth. ☐   **2** This is an ear. ☐

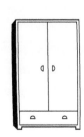

3 This is a window. ☐   **4** This is a top. ☐

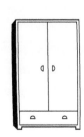

5 These are games consoles. ☐   **6** This is a wardrobe. ☐

☐ / ⑥

Part 2 Reading and Writing

Look at the pictures. Look at the letters. Write the words.

Example

0 s c i s s o r s

Questions

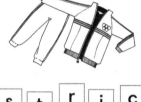
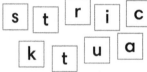

1 _ _ _ _ _ _ _ _ _   **2** _ _ _ _ _ _ _ _

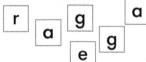

3 _ _ _ _ _ _   **4** _ _ _ _ _ _ _

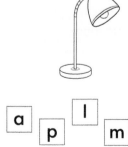

5 _ _ _ _ _ _ _ _   **6** _ _ _ _

☐ / ⑥

name _____   class _____

Part 3 Reading and Writing

Look and read. Write **yes** or **no**.

Examples

0 There are two children in the kitchen.   _yes_

0 The fish is on the table.   _no_

Questions

1 Dad is in front of the fridge.   _____

2 Mum has got long, straight, blond hair.   _____

3 The dog is under the table.   _____

4 The girl has got a shirt and a jumper.   _____

5 There are two plants in the kitchen.   _____

6 There are four chairs and a table in the kitchen.   _____

☐ / ⑥

name _____ class _____

Part 4 Listening and Communication

🔊 **12** Look at the picture. Listen and colour. There is one example.

☐ / 6

name _____ class _____

Part 5 Listening and Communication

Look at the pictures of people at Gerry's house. Draw a line from the pictures to the correct sentences. Look at the pictures very carefully. There are two extra sentences.

Hello. Please come in.

Dad, this is Jenny.

No, thank you.

I'm sorry about that!

Be careful!

That's all right.

The bathroom is upstairs.

Where are you from?

Would you like a sandwich?

☐ / 6

Reading and Writing ☐ / 18
Listening and Communication ☐ / 12
Your total score ☐ / 30

name _____   class _____

Part 1 Reading and Writing

Read and complete. Choose from the box. There is one extra picture. There is one example.

Jake is sporty and very healthy. He gets up ⁰*early* every morning. He eats
fruit and ¹_____ and he ²_____ a lot of water.
He always ³_____ his teeth after meals. He goes
⁴_____ before school. Then he has a ⁵_____ .
On Saturdays and Sundays he plays ⁶_____ with his friends.
When the weather is ⁷_____ and sunny, he goes swimming.
In the winter, when it's ⁸_____ , he goes skiing.

Example

early

hot

vegetables

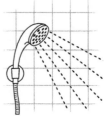

shower

drinks

snowy

brushes

running

tennis

taekwondo

☐ / 8

name _____   class _____

Part 2 Reading and Writing

Look at the pictures and read the questions. Write one-word answers.

Example

0 Where are the people?
at *school*

Questions

1 What can the boy and girl do?

_____

2 How many actors can you see?

_____

3 What can the teacher play?
the _____

4 What can the boy and girl do?

_____

5 Where are the boy and the girl?
_____ to the teacher

Holloway School

The Boyfriend

19–21 July,
7 o'clock

Tickets:
£ 2.00

6 What is on the wall?
a _____

7 Whose shoe has the dog got?
the _____

8 Where is the man?
_____ the door

/ 8

name _____   class _____

Part 3 Listening and Communication

🔊 **13** Read the questions. Look at the picture. Listen and write a word or a number. There is one example.

Example

0 What is the tortoise's name?   *Garibaldi*

Questions

1 Where is the tortoise from?   _____

2 How old is he?   _____

3 What does he eat?   _____

4 What kind of food is bad for him?   _____

5 What can he do?   _____

6 What does he like doing?   _____ in the sun

7 What does he hate?   _____ weather

◻ / ⑦

name _____   class _____

Part 4 Listening and Communication

Read the text. Choose the correct answer.

Example

0 Luke: Hello, Gina. Please come in.

Gina: **a** Thank you.

  b I'm OK.

  c I'm fine, thanks.

Questions

1 Luke: Would you like a cupcake?

Gina: **a** Yes, I do.

  b I like it.

  c Yes, please.

2 Gina: Oh no! The cake is on the floor! I'm so sorry!

Luke: **a** Where is it?

  b No problem.

  c They're all right.

3 Gina: Where's the bathroom, please?

Luke: **a** It's upstairs, next to my bedroom.

  b Here you are.

  c Yes, you can.

4 Luke: Let's do something fun!

Gina: **a** Great idea.

  b No, we don't.

  c Yes, it is.

5 Luke: We can go ice-skating.

Gina: **a** Let me show you.

  b Can you help me?

  c It's not a good idea.

6 Luke: What's your favourite activity?

Gina: **a** I hate swimming.

  b My favourite sports person is Ronaldo.

  c I love watching films.

7 Luke: What time is the film on TV?

Gina: **a** In the summer.

  b It's at eight o'clock.

  c It's five.

☐ / ⑦

Reading and Writing	☐ / ⑯
Listening and Communication	☐ / ⑭
Your total score	☐ / ㉚

1&2 Speaking Tasks

Notes for the teacher

- **Vocabulary:** family members, ages, clothes, adjectives to describe clothes, nationalities and places,
- **Grammar:** utterances using the verb *to be*, demonstrative pronouns and adjectives, possessive adjectives.

Task 1: Ask the student to look at the picture. Then ask the questions.

- This is Kevin and his family. Are they in the garden?
- Where are they?
- How old is Kevin?
- Who is Emma/Charles etc.? [To elicit family members]
- What's this/that/these/those? [To elicit clothes]
- Look at Kevin. Where are Kevin and his family from?
- Where is Giorgio from?
- What's this/that? [To elicit objects]

Task 2: Ask the student to talk about himself/ herself. Use these questions to help.

- How old are you?
- Where are you from?
- What are your favourite clothes?
- What are your favourite things?

4 Speaking Tasks

Notes for the teacher

- **Vocabulary:** rooms of the house and household objects; prepositions of place; vocabulary to describe the face, body and hair; adjectives to describe people,
- **Grammar:** utterances using the verb *to be*, *have got*, *there is/there are*, possessive adjectives.

Task 1: Ask the student to look at the picture. Then ask the questions.

- This is a picture of Amanda and her brothers, Alfie and Richard. Tell me about Amanda's face and hair.
- Tell me about Alfie's face and hair.
- What rooms are there in the house?
- What is there in the bathroom/bedroom/living room/kitchen of the toy house?
- Is there a (plant) in the (living room)?
- Where's the (wardrobe)?

Task 2: Ask the student to talk about himself/herself. Use these questions to help.

- Tell me about your living room/bedroom.
- Is there a (desk) in (the bedroom)?
- Where's the (television)?
- Who is your best friend? Tell me about your best friend's face and hair.
- Tell me about his/her personality.
- Tell me about your mother's/father's/brother's/sister's/etc. face and hair.
- Tell me about his/her personality.

85

5&6 Speaking Tasks

Notes for the teacher

- **Vocabulary:** verbs; collocations with *make*, *play* and *ride*; daily activities (days of the week, months, time),
- **Grammar:** utterances using *can*, the Present Simple (and the Present Simple with adverbs of frequency).

Task 1: Ask the student to look at the picture. Then ask the questions.

- These are pictures of Eric and his family. What can Eric do?
- What can Eric's dad do?
- What can Eric's mum do?
- Can Eric's dad ride a bike?
- Tell me about Eric's morning.
- Tell me about Eric's afternoon.
- Tell me about Eric's parents' evening.

Task 2: Ask the student to talk about himself/ herself. Use these questions to help.

- What do you do in the morning, afternoon and evening?
- What does your mum /dad do in the morning, afternoon and evening?
- Tell me about your weekend.
- Can you ride a bike?
- What can you do?
- What can your best friend do?

Summer Camp

Activities for children 10–16

✔ What do you do in the summer holidays?

✔ Do you get up late and watch TV or play computer games?

✔ Don't be boring! This year do some fun activities – and get healthy!

8 Speaking Tasks

Notes for the teacher

- **Vocabulary:** sports, healthy lifestyle (pets, wild animals),
- **Grammar:** utterances using the Present Simple, *love/like/don't like/hate + -ing.*

Task 1: Ask the student to look at the picture. Then ask the questions.

- When is the camp?
- Who goes to the camp?
- What sports do children play at the summer camp?
- What water sports do they do?
- Do they do any team or ball sports?
- Can children ride a horse at the summer camp?
- Can children play computer games at the summer camp?

Task 2: Ask the student to talk about himself/herself. Use these questions to help.

- What do you do in the summer holidays?
- Are you sporty?
- What sports do you do?
- What activities don't you like doing?
- Have you got a pet?
- Tell me about your pet.

1-8 Writing Tasks

Unit 1 Family and friends

Write 40–50 words about you and your family. Use questions 1–5 to help you.

1 What is your name? How old are you?
2 Where are you from?
3 Who is in your family? What are their names?
4 How old are they?
5 Where are they now?

Unit 2 My things

Write 40–50 words about your friend. Use questions 1–5 to help you.

1 What is your friend's name?
2 Where is he/she from?
3 What is his/her favourite colour?
4 Who is his/her favourite actor/singer?
5 Describe three of his/her favourite things.

Unit 3 In the house

Write 40–50 words about your favourite room. Use questions 1–5 to help you.

1 What is your favourite room?
2 What things are there in your room?
3 What colour are they?
4 Where are the things?
5 What's your favourite thing in the room?

Unit 4 About me

Write 40–50 words about a person in your family or in your class. Use questions 1–5 to help you.

1 Is he/she tall or short?
2 Write about his/her face.
3 Write about his/her hair.
4 Write about his/her personality.
5 What is his/her hobby?

Unit 5 Things I can do

Write 40–50 words about what you and your family *can* and *can't* do. Use questions 1–5 to help you.

1 Are you and your family talented?
2 What things can you do?
3 What things can't you do?
4 What can your mother/father/sister/brother/grandma/grandpa do?
5 What things can't he/she do?

Unit 6 My day

Write 40–70 words about what you and your family do in your summer holidays. Use questions 1–6 to help you.

1 When are the summer holidays?
2 What time do you usually get up?
3 What do you do in the morning?
4 What do you do in the afternoon?
5 What do you do in the evening?
6 What time do you go to bed?

Unit 7 Animals

Write 40–70 words about your favourite animals. Use questions 1–6 to help you.

1 What are your favourite animals?
2 Can you see them in the zoo/in the park/in the garden/in the sea?
3 Write about their body (e.g. eyes, ears, mouth, teeth, nose, legs).
4 What can they do?
5 What do they eat?
6 What do they like?

Unit 8 I like that!

Write 40–70 words about a summer camp for sports. Use questions 1–6 to help you.

1 Where is the summer camp?
2 When do you go to the camp?
3 What sports can you do there?
4 What sports can't you do there?
5 What sports do you like doing?
6 What do you do when it is rainy?

Audio script

2 Skills Test 1&2
Exercise 1

M: man MT: Mateo

M: Hello. I'm Dan. I'm your new neighbour. What's your name?
MT: Hi. My name's Mateo.
M: Are you Italian?
MT: No, I'm not. I'm Spanish, but my friend Gabriella is from Italy.
M: How old are you?
MT: I'm eleven and Gabriella is twelve.
M: Who are those children?
MT: That's Peter.
M: Is he British?
MT: No, he's American. And that's Anna. She's Chinese.
M: Anna? Is that a Chinese name?
MT: No, it isn't. Anna's dad is Chinese but her mum is Polish.

3 Skills Test 1&2
Exercise 2

G1: girl G2: girl

G1: … Oh, no! Bad dog, Rover! Look at these clothes!
G2: Are these your boots?
G1: No, they're too big. They're John's.
G2: And this brown coat?
G1: It's Granny's coat. It's boring. Hmm … That pink and white dress isn't my sister's … It's my mum's dress.
G2: This red and purple hoodie is cool.
G1: Yes, it's my sister's. And these are my new jeans.
G2: They're too long.
G1: I know, but I love them. And my orange shirt. Orange is my favourite colour!

4 Skills Test 3&4
Exercise 1

G: girl

G: This is our living room. It isn't big, but it's nice. There's a carpet in the living room. There's a television on the wall. There's a table in front of the sofa and there are two cushions on the sofa. A big lamp is next to the armchair, and look! My book is under the sofa! There's a plant next to the window. My dog Pippin is under the desk and there's a chair in front of the desk. What else? There's a skateboard behind the door. And my brother's backpack is behind the door too.

5 Skills Test 3&4
Exercise 2

B: boy G: girl

G: Who's that girl in the photo?
B: My cousin Darla. She isn't British. She's Irish, from Dublin, in Ireland. She's 13 years old.
G: She's got a long face …
B: … and green eyes. Her teeth are white and she's got curly red hair. She's very tall and she's got long legs. Darla is helpful and she talks to everybody. She's clever too and she gets good marks at school.
G: And that little dog?
B: That's Darla's dog. His name is Frisky. He's got big brown eyes, short legs and short, black and white hair.
G: He's got a funny little face!

6 Skills Test 5&6
Exercise 1

N: narrator M: man G/J/Sh/E: girl/Julie/Sarah/Ellen A/S/B: Adam/Sam/boy

N: Example.
N: What can Adam do?
G: Can you cook, Adam?
A: No, I can't. And I can't make cakes.
G: What can you do?
A: I can draw pictures. Look!
N: One.
N: Where is Sam's sister?
J: Hi, Sam. Where's your brother?
S: My brother isn't at home today. He plays tennis at school on Tuesdays.
J: And your sister?
S: She's in the park. She always hangs out with her friends there in the afternoon.
N: Two.
N: What can Mark play?
G: Who's that boy?
Sh: That's my cousin Mark. He can't play football and he can't skateboard. But he's a fantastic pianist. He can play the piano well!
A: I can't play the piano – but I can play football!
N: Three.
N: What club is on Wednesday?
B: Have we got Diving Club on Monday?
G: No, we haven't. We've got Music Club on Monday. Diving Club is on Wednesday.
B: And when's Art Club?
G: It's on Friday.
N: Four.
N: What time is the football match on TV?
G: What time is it?
M: It's half past five.
G: The match is on TV at quarter to six.

M: No, it isn't. The film is at quarter to six. The match is at quarter to eight.
N: Five.
N: What does Ellen's dad do in the evening?
B: Ellen, what do you and your family do in the evening?
E: Well, I sometimes watch TV.
B: What about your parents?
E: Well, Dad usually plays computer games with me, but Mum hates them. She reads her book.

7 Skills Test 5&6
Exercise 2

G: girl

G: What can my family do? Well, Mum can fix things. She fixes our car and our bikes! She can cook and she makes dinner every day. Dad can cook too. He makes breakfast for the family every weekend. But Dad is a very bad singer. He sings in the shower and my brother always shouts: 'Be quiet, Dad!' Granny Sophie is Dad's mum, but she can sing well. She can play the piano too. Grandad Alex can't sing or play the piano, but he can draw fantastic pictures. My brother Louis is sporty and he loves football. He plays football for the school and he watches all the football matches on TV on Sundays.

8 Skills Test 7&8
Exercise 1

B: boy G: girl

B: Hey, Rachel, look at these photos of my American friends on my mobile phone. They're from my holiday. This funny photo is my favourite.
G: Who's the boy?
B: My cousin Martin and that's his cat Moggy. They always get up late on holiday. … That's my friend Monique.
G: Is Monique the girl with long blond hair?
B: Yes. She goes skateboarding every day. … And this is Tony.
G: These tortoises are big! Is Tony the boy next to the tortoise?
B: No, that's his little brother Mac.
G: Who's that?
B: That's Irek. He's from Poland, but now he lives in the USA. He does a lot of exercise and he's very healthy.
G: That's a great photo. Where's this beach?
B: In California. My friend Cilla lives there.
G: Lucky Cilla! Is that her?
B: Yes. She goes swimming every day. … And here's Diana and me at the zoo.
G: The parrots are fantastic! Your photos are great!

Audio script

🔊 **9 Skills Test 7&8**
Exercise 2

B: boy

B: These are my dogs, Sidney and Gertie. Sidney is a black Labrador and Gertie is a cute brown Chihuahua. Sidney and Gertie are my best friends. I take them for a walk every morning before breakfast and every evening before dinner. They love running after rabbits in the park. Sidney likes swimming in the sea but Gertie hates the water. Sidney eats a lot of food – he's a big dog. Gertie doesn't eat a lot because she's very small.
Sidney and Gertie aren't the only animals in the house. There's also my mum's cat, Ginger. Ginger doesn't like the dogs and the dogs don't like her. She loves sleeping on the sofa and watching the birds in the garden!

🔊 **10 Mid-Year Test 1–4**
Exercise 7

M: Michael A: Aunt

A: Hi, Michael!
M: Hi, Aunt Fran.
A: Who are those people in the garden?
M: They're our new neighbours, Mr and Mrs Jenkins. The boy with short black hair is their son, Jack. He's fourteen.
A: And the little boy with dark spiky hair?
M: His name's Tom. He's Jack's brother. He's only six.
A: And the girl with long wavy brown hair?
M: That's Jenny. She's eleven years old and she's in my class at school.

🔊 **11 End-of-Year Test 1–8**
Exercise 7

G: girl B: boy

G: Henry loves getting up early. He gets up at six o'clock and goes running. Then at half past seven he has breakfast. Henry rides his bike to school. He loves cycling. He's sporty and he plays football for the school. He wants to play football for Manchester United. Henry can run fast and dive. He often plays hockey too.
B: Rosie hates getting up early. She's often late for school! But Rosie is clever. She gets good marks at school. She can draw animals and she can write stories. She wants to be an actor and go to Hollywood. She can act and she can dance but she can't sing.

🔊 **12 Exam Test 1–4**
Part 4

N: narrator M: man G: girl

N: Look at the picture. Listen and colour. There is one example.
G: There are a lot of chairs here!
M: Yes. There's an armchair next to the house. There's a cat on it.
G: Next to the house? A cat?
M: Yes. Colour the armchair GREY.
G: OK, grey.
N: Can you see the grey armchair? This is an example. Now you listen and colour.
N: One
M: There's a chair under the tree.
G: Is there a skateboard next to it?
M: Yes, there is. Colour that chair YELLOW.
G: OK. Yellow is a good colour.
N: Two
M: There's a chair behind that table.
G: And a cushion on the chair.
M: Colour that chair PURPLE.
G: Purple?
M: Yes, please.
N: Three
M: That tall man is next to a long chair!
G: He's a very tall man!
M: Please colour the long chair ORANGE.
G: Orange. Good.
N: Four
M: That chair has got three legs.
G: Three legs! It isn't a good chair!
M: No, it isn't. Colour that chair BLUE.
G: Blue is cool.
M: Thank you.
N: Five
M: One of the chairs is small. There's a small dog behind it.
G: The dog's got a long body!
M: Colour that chair GREEN.
G: Right. Green.
N: Six
M: Look at the chair with the baby.
G: Is it near the house?
M: Yes, it is. Colour that chair PINK.
G: Pink is nice.
N: Now listen to part 4 again.

🔊 **13 Exam Test 5–8**
Part 3

N: narrator M: Maggie UP: Uncle Pete

N: Look at the picture. Listen and write a word or a number. There is one example.
M: Hi, Uncle Pete. Is that your tortoise?
UP: Yes, it is.
M: What's his name?
UP: Garibaldi.
M: How do you spell … Garibaldi?
UP: Garibaldi. G-A-R-I-B-A-L-D-I.
N: Can you see the answer? Now you listen and write a word or a number.
N: One
M: Garibaldi is a funny name!
UP: Well, Garibaldi is an Italian name, and Garibaldi is from Italy!
N: Two
M: How old is he?
UP: He's thirty-six!
M: 36! That's old!
N: Three
M: What does he eat?
UP: He eats plants.
N: Four
M: Does he eat fruit too?
UP: No, he doesn't. Fruit is bad for tortoises!
N: Five
M: What can he do?
UP: Well, he can't swim, but he can climb!
M: He can?
UP: Yes, he can!
N: Six
M: What does he like doing?
UP: Sitting in the sun.
N: Seven
M: I like sitting in the sun too. I don't like cold weather.
UP: Well, Garibaldi hates cold weather too.
N: Look and listen again.

Answer key

Placement Test

Exercise 1
A: 1 family 2 China 3 lesson 4 skateboard 5 classroom
B: 1 family 2 Spain 3 floor 4 skateboard 5 classroom

Exercise 2
A: 1 rabbit 2 teeth 3 legs 4 monkey 5 giraffe
B: 1 legs 2 giraffe 3 monkey 4 teeth 5 rabbit

Exercise 3
A: 1 go 2 drink 3 do 4 listen 5 have
B: 1 do 2 have 3 eat 4 go 5 watch

Exercise 4
A: 1 draw 2 clever 3 console 4 hamster 5 cute
B: 1 play 2 clever 3 mountain 4 hamster 5 cute

Exercise 5
A: 1 is 2 Their 3 those 4 Am I 5 his
B: 1 is 2 that 3 their 4 her 5 Am I

Exercise 6
A: 1 b 2 e 3 c 4 a 5 d
B: 1 e 2 b 3 c 4 a 5 d

Exercise 7
A: 1 What can we do at the museum? 2 My parents don't go to work on Sundays. 3 There aren't any trees in the garden. 4 Where do your aunt and uncle live? 5 Susan always watches TV in the evening.
B: 1 What can we do at the museum? 2 When does the lesson finish? 3 My friends don't go to school on Saturdays. 4 Luke never watches television in the evening. 5 There aren't any cushions on the sofa.

Exercise 8
A: 1 c 2 b 3 c 4 a 5 a
B: 1 b 2 c 3 a 4 c 5 a

Exercise 9
A: 1 a 2 c 3 c 4 a 5 b
B: 1 b 2 c 3 b 4 a 5 b

Exercise 10
A: 1 Let 2 fine 3 idea 4 have 5 Here
B: 1 idea 2 show 3 please 4 Here 5 fine

Vocabulary Check 1

Exercise 1
A: 1 father 2 grandmother 3 grandfather 4 son 5 daughter 6 uncle 7 aunt 8 brother 9 sister 10 cousin
B: 1 father 2 sister 3 brother 4 aunt 5 uncle 6 grandfather 7 grandmother 8 daughter 9 son 10 cousin

Exercise 2
A: 1 France 2 Chinese 3 Poland 4 American 5 Italy
B: 1 Spain 2 American 3 Italy 4 Polish 5 China

Exercise 3
A: 1 in 2 at 3 at 4 on 5 in
B: 1 on 2 at 3 in 4 at 5 in

Vocabulary Check 2

Exercise 1
A: 1 jacket 2 skirt 3 cap 4 shirt 5 jumper 6 trousers 7 dress 8 coat 9 hoodie 10 trainers
B: 1 skirt 2 cap 3 shirt 4 jumper 5 shoes 6 coat 7 dress 8 boots 9 hoodie 10 jeans

Exercise 2
A: 1 small 2 new 3 short 4 boring 5 big
B: 1 small 2 cool 3 short 4 big 5 old

Exercise 3
A: 1 mobile 2 skateboard 3 mountain 4 console 5 backpack
B: 1 mountain 2 console 3 backpack 4 mobile 5 skateboard

Vocabulary Check 3

Exercise 1
A: 1 wardrobe 2 door 3 bath 4 living room 5 sofa 6 table 7 fridge 8 chair 9 garage 10 garden
B: 1 desk 2 chair 3 window 4 bathroom 5 armchair 6 table 7 floor 8 wall 9 kitchen 10 garage

Exercise 2
A: 1 d 2 e 3 a 4 b 5 c
B: 1 b 2 a 3 d 4 e 5 c

Exercise 3
A: 1 carpet 2 plant 3 lamp 4 cushion 5 poster
B: 1 cushion 2 plant 3 carpet 4 poster 5 lamp

Vocabulary Check 4

Exercise 1
A: 1 ears 2 eyes 3 mouth 4 teeth 5 nose 6 curly 7 wavy 8 blond 9 straight 10 dark
B: 1 eyes 2 straight 3 dark 4 nose 5 ears 6 mouth 7 teeth 8 curly 9 wavy 10 blond

Exercise 2
A: 1 neck 2 toes 3 foot 4 fingers 5 hand
B: 1 arm 2 fingers 3 head 4 toes 5 leg

Vocabulary Check 5

Exercise 1
A: 1 draw 2 dive 3 swim 4 act 5 fix 6 run 7 jump 8 fly 9 cook 10 skateboard
B: 1 draw 2 fly 3 run 4 jump 5 cook 6 skateboard 7 act 8 fix 9 dive 10 swim

Exercise 2
A: 1 read 2 write 3 climb 4 ride 5 sing
B: 1 sing 2 read 3 ride 4 climb 5 write

Exercise 3
A: 1 b 2 c 3 a 4 d 5 e
B: 1 c 2 b 3 e 4 d 5 a

Vocabulary Check 6

Exercise 1
A: 1 have 2 have 3 hang 4 have 5 watch 6 listen 7 get 8 go 9 tidy 10 do
B: 1 listen 2 have 3 watch 4 hang 5 have 6 have 7 do 8 get 9 tidy 10 go

Exercise 2
A: 1 Fridays 2 Wednesdays 3 Thursdays 4 Saturdays 5 Mondays
B: 1 Mondays 2 Thursdays 3 Wednesdays 4 Saturdays 5 Sundays

Exercise 3
A: 1 August 2 February 3 April 4 October 5 June
B: 1 January 2 July 3 May 4 September 5 December

Vocabulary Check 7

Exercise 1
A: 1 monkey 2 snake 3 kangaroo 4 butterfly 5 spider 6 frog 7 fish 8 whale 9 giraffe 10 crocodile
B: 1 snake 2 lion 3 giraffe 4 elephant 5 crocodile 6 bird 7 spider 8 frog 9 whale 10 kangaroo

Exercise 2
A: 1 d 2 a 3 c 4 b 5 e
B: 1 d 2 a 3 c 4 b 5 f

Exercise 3
A: 1 cute 2 dangerous 3 slow 4 strong 5 ugly
B: 1 strong 2 cute 3 ugly 4 slow 5 dangerous

Vocabulary Check 8

Exercise 1
A: 1 badminton 2 hockey 3 windsurfing 4 roller skating 5 cycling 6 table tennis 7 ice-skating 8 basketball 9 sailing 10 skiing
B: 1 basketball 2 ice-skating 3 hockey 4 badminton 5 sailing 6 windsurfing 7 skiing 8 table tennis 9 roller skating 10 cycling

Exercise 2
A: 1 do 2 play 3 go 4 go 5 play
B: 1 go 2 play 3 do 4 play 5 go

Exercise 3
A: 1 Brush 2 Drink 3 Eat 4 Do 5 Have
B: 1 Do 2 Eat 3 Drink 4 Brush 5 Have

Grammar Check 1

Exercise 1
A: 1 are 2 am 3 are 4 is 5 are
B: 1 are 2 are 3 is 4 am 5 is

Exercise 2
A: 1 her 2 his 3 Magda's 4 my 5 your
B: 1 my 2 Her 3 your 4 his 5 Julie's

Exercise 3
A: 1 aren't 2 aren't 3 'm not 4 aren't 5 isn't
B: 1 aren't 2 aren't 3 isn't 4 aren't 5 'm not

Grammar Check 2

Exercise 1
A: 1 These 2 Those 3 That 4 This 5 Those
B: 1 Those 2 These 3 This 4 That 5 Those

Exercise 2
A: 1 Are they in the park? 2 What is your favourite colour? 3 Am I boring? 4 Are you a superhero? 5 Is she Anna's best friend?
B: 1 Am I your best friend? 2 Are you Superdug's brother? 3 Are they long trousers? 4 Is he a superhero? 5 What is your favourite film?

Exercise 3
A: 1 I am 2 you are 3 it isn't 4 we aren't 5 they are
B: 1 they are 2 I'm not 3 we are 4 you are 5 it isn't

Grammar Check 3

Exercise 1
A: 1 There are 2 There's 3 There are 4 There are 5 There's
B: 1 There are 2 There are 3 There's 4 There's 5 There are

91

Answer key

Exercise 2
A: 1 There aren't two armchairs in the bedroom. 2 There aren't four apple trees in the garden. 3 There isn't a bag on the floor. 4 There isn't a computer on the table.

B: 1 There aren't four girls in your family. 2 There aren't two cars in the garage. 3 There isn't a poster on the wall. 4 There isn't a phone on the table.

Exercise 3
A: 1 Are 2 are 3 there 4 No 5 Is 6 Yes

B: 1 Are 2 aren't 3 there 4 No 5 Is 6 Yes

Grammar Check 4
Exercise 1
A: 1 has got 2 haven't got 3 hasn't got 4 haven't got 5 have got

B: 1 has got 2 haven't got 3 haven't got 4 hasn't got 5 have got

Exercise 2
A: 1 Has 2 hasn't 3 got 4 have 5 Have 6 haven't

B: 1 got 2 No 3 Has 4 hasn't 5 Have 6 have

Exercise 3
A: 1 Its 2 Their 3 Our 4 Your

B: 1 Their 2 Its 3 Your 4 Our

Grammar Check 5
Exercise 1
A: 1 My mother can make great cupcakes. 2 I can fix the television. 3 Clara and her best friend can't speak English. 4 Superdug can't do clever things with computers. 5 My brother and I can play the piano.

B: 1 Max and his best friend can't speak English. 2 My sister and I can play the guitar. 3 His aunt can't make cakes. 4 Kit's friend can do clever things with computers. 5 I can't fix the radio.

Exercise 2
A: 1 Can Jack and I go home? 2 Can your dad fix this camera? 3 What can your mum do? 4 Can the students read difficult words? 5 Can Betty's dog run fast?

B: 1 Can the students write good stories? 2 Can your brother fix that computer? 3 Can Molly and I go home? 4 Can Ryan's horse run fast? 5 What can your best friend do?

Exercise 3
A: 1 No, they can't. 2 Yes, he can. 3 No, it can't. 4 Yes, you can. 5 No, we can't.

B: 1 Yes, they can. 2 No, we can't. 3 Yes, she can. 4 No, he can't. 5 Yes, you can.

Grammar Check 6
Exercise 1
A: 1 hang 2 listens 3 cooks 4 draw 5 run

B: 1 climb 2 listens 3 hang 4 plays 5 draw

Exercise 2
A: 1 has 2 makes 3 fixes 4 does 5 tidies

B: 1 fixes 2 tidies 3 does 4 makes 5 has

Exercise 3
A: 1 My classmates and I always do our homework. 2 Nesta often listens to music. 3 The boys sometimes play football. 4 My grandad usually goes to bed early. 5 Ania and Ewa are never late on Thursday.

B: 1 The girls sometimes play tennis. 2 My friends and I always do our homework. 3 My parents usually go to work early. 4 Julia and her sisters are never late on Tuesday. 5 Gerry often listens to music.

Grammar Check 7
Exercise 1
A: 1 doesn't feed 2 don't like 3 doesn't have 4 don't walk 5 doesn't take

B: 1 don't do 2 doesn't run 3 doesn't cook 4 don't like 5 doesn't get

Exercise 2
A: 1 Do these animals live in Africa? 2 Does Superdug have dinner with Kit? 3 Does your sister tidy her bedroom on Saturdays? 4 Do Alex and Jane watch TV in the evening? 5 Does his mother get up early?

B: 1 Does your dad tidy his room on Mondays? 2 Does her brother go to bed late? 3 Does Kit have lunch with Superdug? 4 Do those animals live in India? 5 Do Suzie and Pete often listen to music?

Exercise 3
A: 1 No, she doesn't. 2 No, they don't. 3 Yes, he does. 4 Yes, we do. 5 No, it doesn't.

B: 1 Yes, he does. 2 No, they don't. 3 Yes, he does. 4 No, it doesn't. 5 Yes, we do.

Grammar Check 8
Exercise 1
A: 1 swimming 2 singing 3 doing 4 running 5 writing

B: 1 cooking 2 reading 3 riding 4 running 5 swimming

Exercise 2
A: 1 it 2 her 3 me 4 them 5 us

B: 1 me 2 it 3 him 4 us 5 them

Exercise 3
A: 1 b 2 d 3 c 4 e 5 a

B: 1 f 2 a 3 e 4 b 5 c

Language Test
Get started!
Exercise 1
A: 1 eleven 2 fourteen 3 forty-three 4 seventy-five 5 a hundred

B: 1 twelve 2 sixty-seven 3 fourteen 4 forty-six 5 a hundred

Exercise 2
A: 1 clock 2 board 3 pencil case 4 rubber 5 scissors

B: 1 rubber 2 board 3 clock 4 scissors 5 pencil case

Exercise 3
A: 1 black 2 green 3 yellow 4 pink 5 grey

B: 1 grey 2 yellow 3 green 4 white 5 pink

Exercise 4
A: 1 an 2 a 3 a 4 an 5 an

B: 1 a 2 an 3 an 4 a 5 an

Exercise 5
A: 1 They're sandwiches. 2 They're pencil cases. 3 They're oranges. 4 They're boxes. 5 They're desks.

B: 1 They're computer games. 2 They're umbrellas. 3 They're sandwiches. 4 They're chairs. 5 They're boxes.

Exercise 6
A: 1 a 2 c 3 b 4 e 5 d

B: 1 b 2 d 3 e 4 c 5 a

Language Test 1
Exercise 1
A: 1 aunt 2 uncle 3 brother 4 daughter 5 son

B: 1 aunt 2 uncle 3 brother 4 daughter 5 son

Exercise 2
A: 1 park 2 UK 3 on 4 American 5 school 6 Poland

B: 1 home 2 American 3 on 4 British 5 in 6 France

Exercise 3
A: 1 'm not 2 is 3 aren't 4 are 5 isn't 6 are

B: 1 aren't 2 is 3 are 4 'm not 5 isn't 6 are

Exercise 4
A: 1 My 2 His 3 your 4 Her

B: 1 your 2 My 3 His 4 Her

Exercise 5
A: 1 Gus's mum is Dido. 2 Fifi is Kiki's sister. 3 Fifi's cousins are Stumpy and Polo. 4 Gizmo and Mitzi are Polo's parents.

B: 1 Lino's mum is Hippy. 2 Dalia is Petunia's sister. 3 Pico's cousins are Dalia, Petunia and Tiberius. 4 Oscar and Hippy are Lino's parents.

Exercise 6
A: 1 Dad, this is Gordon. 2 He's my classmate. 3 Gordon, this is my dad. 4 Hello, Gordon. 5 Nice to meet you. 6 Nice to meet you too.

B: 1 Mum, this is Ivy. 2 She's my friend. 3 Ivy, this is my mum. 4 Hello, Ivy. 5 Nice to meet you. 6 Nice to meet you too.

Language Test 2
Exercise 1
A: 1 skirt 2 short 3 jumper 4 boring 5 too 6 tracksuit 7 new

B: 1 cool 2 hoodie 3 old 4 too 5 trainers 6 jacket 7 skirt

Exercise 2
A: 1 games console 2 mobile phone 3 skateboard 4 backpack

B: 1 mountain bike 2 backpack 3 games console 4 skateboard

Exercise 3
A: 1 These 2 Those 3 That 4 This

B: 1 That 2 These 3 Those 4 This

Exercise 4
A: 1 Are they best friends? 2 Is he Olivia's cousin? 3 Are those new comic books for me? 4 Where is she from? 5 Are you in the park?

B: 1 How old is he? 2 Are they good students? 3 Are you in the garden? 4 Are these old comic books for me? 5 Is she Joe's aunt?

Exercise 5
A: 1 No, he isn't. 2 Yes, it is. 3 No, we aren't. 4 Yes, they are. 5 Yes, she is.

B: 1 Yes, we are. 2 No, he isn't. 3 No, they aren't. 4 Yes, she is. 5 No, it isn't.

Exercise 6
A: 1 Where 2 old 3 years 4 Who 5 what

B: 1 old 2 years 3 from 4 What 5 Who

Answer key

Language Test 3

Exercise 1
A: 1 sofa 2 cushions
3 armchair 4 wardrobe
5 carpet 6 lamps
B: 1 wardrobe 2 floor
3 tables 4 lamps 5 sofa
6 armchair

Exercise 2
A: 1 on 2 under 3 next
4 in front
B: 1 next 2 under 3 behind
4 on

Exercise 3
A: 1 There are 2 Is there
3 There aren't 4 There is
5 There isn't 6 Are there
B: 1 There isn't 2 Are there
3 There aren't 4 There is
5 Is there 6 There are

Exercise 4
A: 1 There isn't a ruler on the
table. 2 Are there any
students in the classroom?
3 Is there a television in your
bedroom? 4 There are four
eggs in the fridge.
B: 1 There isn't a pencil in the
pencil case. 2 Is there a
games console in the living
room? 3 There aren't any
apples on the tree. 4 Are
there any oranges in the
kitchen?

Exercise 5
A: 1 any 2 any 3 There 4 a
5 isn't
B: 1 any 2 are 3 any 4 there
5 a

Exercise 6
A: 1 Would 2 please
3 Where's 4 upstairs 5 Let
B: 1 like 2 thank 3 Where's
4 downstairs 5 show

Language Test 4

Exercise 1
A: 1 neck 2 legs 3 fingers
4 hands 5 toes 6 feet
B: 1 body 2 mouth 3 tooth
4 toes 5 fingers 6 hands

Exercise 2
A: 1 sporty 2 nice 3 clever
4 funny
B: 1 funny 2 sporty 3 nice
4 friendly

Exercise 3
A: 1 haven't got 2 hasn't got
3 has got 4 have got
B: 1 hasn't got 2 haven't got
3 have got 4 has got

Exercise 4
A: 1 have 2 Has 3 hasn't
4 got 5 they 6 have
7 haven't
B: 1 haven't 2 got 3 they
4 Has 5 hasn't 6 have
7 have

Exercise 5
A: 1 Our eyes 2 Its battery
3 Your house 4 Their teacher
B: 1 Its garden 2 Our eyes
3 Their students 4 Your marks

Exercise 6
A: 1 so 2 about 3 all
4 mistake 5 No
B: 1 mistake 2 No 3 about
4 all 5 so

Language Test 5

Exercise 1
A: 1 sing 2 climb 3 swim
4 dive 5 cook 6 jump
B: 1 swim 2 dive 3 jump
4 climb 5 skateboard
6 sing

Exercise 2
A: 1 fix 2 draw 3 play 4 ride
5 play
B: 1 draw 2 fix 3 play 4 ride
5 play

Exercise 3
A: 1 Elephants can't jump.
2 Cats can't sing songs.
3 Zebras can run fast.
4 Dogs can't climb trees.
B: 1 Cats can climb trees.
2 Elephants can't dive.
3 Dogs can't sing songs.
4 Zebras can run fast.

Exercise 4
A: 1 Can Freddie skateboard
here? 2 Can Marcus play
tennis? 3 What can Dave
cook? 4 Can Amy see two
boats?
B: 1 Can Freddie play tennis?
2 What can Marcus write?
3 Can Sam make posters?
4 Can Barbara and Evan
play football?

Exercise 5
A: 1 Can 2 can't 3 Can
4 she 5 can 6 What
B: 1 Can 2 can't 3 What
4 Can 5 he 6 can

Exercise 6
A: 1 agree 2 swimming
3 idea 4 can 5 that
B: 1 Any 2 skateboarding
3 idea 4 can 5 do

Language Test 6

Exercise 1
A: 1 Wednesdays 2 get
3 shower 4 do 5 dinner
6 to 7 Saturdays 8 out
B: 1 Thursdays 2 up
3 breakfast 4 do 5 to
6 shower 7 Saturdays 8 with

Exercise 2
A: 1 April 2 June 3 August
4 November
B: 1 May 2 June 3 July
4 October

Exercise 3
A: 1 plays 2 draw 3 runs
4 write 5 climbs
B: 1 write 2 draw 3 plays
4 climbs 5 runs

Exercise 4
A: 1 She has eggs for
breakfast. 2 He tidies his
bedroom every Saturday.
3 She watches TV in the
evening. 4 He fixes cars
and bikes.
B: 1 He tidies the living room
every Saturday. 2 She fixes
bikes and cars. 3 He has
sandwiches for lunch. 4 She
watches TV in the evening.

Exercise 5
A: 1 I always go to bed early
on Monday. 2 I sometimes
watch TV in the evening.
3 I never cook breakfast in
the morning. 4 I usually
read a book in the evening.
B: 1 I never cook dinner in the
evening. 2 I always go to
bed late on Sunday.
3 I usually read a book in
the evening. 4 I sometimes
watch TV after school.

Exercise 6
A: 1 It's at half past five. 2 It's
at nine o'clock. 3 It's at five
to eight. 4 It's at quarter to
one. 5 It's at quarter past
ten.
B: 1 It's at quarter past four.
2 It's at half past eleven.
3 It's at five to ten. 4 It's
at quarter to six. 5 It's at
seven o'clock.

Language Test 7

Exercise 1
A: 1 Crocodiles 2 dangerous
3 Tortoises 4 slow 5 Flies
6 ugly 7 lions 8 cute
B: 1 Tortoises 2 slow
3 Crocodiles 4 dangerous
5 lions 6 cute 7 Flies
8 ugly

Exercise 2
A: 1 frog 2 monkey 3 spider
4 rabbit
B: 1 monkey 2 rabbit 3 frog
4 spider

Exercise 3
A: 1 don't eat 2 doesn't go
3 doesn't do 4 don't watch
B: 1 doesn't go 2 don't listen
3 doesn't ride 4 don't eat

Exercise 4
A: 1 Does your sister get up
early in the morning? 2 Do
the children have lessons
in the afternoon? 3 What
do you do in the evening?
4 What does he draw?
B: 1 Do the students have
lunch at twelve o'clock?
2 Does Lucy go to bed early
on Sundays? 3 What do you
draw? 4 What does she do
in the evening?

Exercise 5
A: 1 do 2 doesn't cook
3 don't help 4 do you do
5 Does Martha play
B: 1 don't 2 doesn't cook
3 don't help 4 do you do
5 Does Zac play

Exercise 6
A: 1 Can 2 have 3 That's
4 you 5 here's
B: 1 Can 2 have 3 That's
4 you 5 here's

Language Test 8

Exercise 1
A: 1 skiing 2 hockey 3 does
4 plays 5 cycling 6 sailing
B: 1 skiing 2 does 3 cycling
4 plays 5 sailing 6 hockey

Exercise 2
A: 1 b 2 b 3 a 4 b 5 a
B: 1 a 2 b 3 b 4 a 5 a

Exercise 3
A: 1 doesn't like 2 going
3 loves 4 getting
B: 1 going 2 loves 3 sitting
4 doesn't like

Exercise 4
A: 1 it 2 them 3 her 4 us
5 me
B: 1 him 2 her 3 it 4 them
5 us

Exercise 5
A: 1 When does she have
lunch? 2 Where does Henry
want to go? 3 What is your
favourite colour? 4 Who do
you love? 5 Whose horse is
it?
B: 1 Who does he love?
2 What is your favourite
colour? 3 Whose dogs are
they? 4 Where do you live?
5 When do they usually have
breakfast?

Exercise 6
A: 1 sunny 2 rainy 3 windy
4 cold 5 snowy
B: 1 snowy 2 sunny 3 hot
4 windy 5 rainy

Skills Test 1&2

Exercise 1
A: 1 T 2 F 3 F 4 T 5 F
B: 1 T 2 F 3 T 4 T 5 F

Exercise 2
A: 1 boring 2 dress 3 cool
4 jeans 5 orange
B: 1 coat 2 pink 3 hoodie
4 long 5 shirt

Exercise 3
A: 1 e 2 d 3 c 4 b 5 a
B: 1 b 2 f 3 e 4 d 5 c

Exercise 4
A: 1 yes 2 no 3 no 4 yes
5 yes
B: 1 no 2 yes 3 no 4 no
5 yes

Answer key

Exercise 5
A: 1 party 2 her 3 aren't 4 from 5 dress
B: 1 his 2 aren't 3 from 4 party 5 jacket

Exercise 6
Model text

> 1 He / She is from the USA / China. 2 He / She is eleven / twelve. 3 His / Her favourite clothes are his T-shirt and his hoodie / her tracksuit and her jeans. 4 His T-shirt is black / Her tracksuit is green. 5 His / Her favourite thing is his skateboard / her mobile phone.

Skills Test 3&4
Exercise 1
A: 1 television – on wall 2 table – in front of sofa 3 book – under sofa 4 plant – next to window (either side) 5 skateboard – behind door
B: 1 cushions – on sofa 2 lamp – next to armchair 3 dog – under the desk 4 chair – in front of the desk 5 backpack – behind door

Exercise 2
A: 1 long 2 curly 3 clever 4 eyes 5 funny
B: 1 eyes 2 long 3 clever 4 short 5 funny

Exercise 3
A: 1 b 2 c 3 c 4 a 5 a
B: 1 b 2 b 3 a 4 a 5 c

Exercise 4
A: 1 T 2 F 3 F 4 T 5 T
B: 1 T 2 F 3 F 4 F 5 T

Exercise 5
A: 1 feet 2 has 3 dark 4 sofa 5 front
B: 1 their 2 has 3 dark 4 carpet 5 next

Exercise 6
Model text

> 1 She is helpful. 2 She's got big, green eyes. 3 Her hair is long, straight and brown. 4 Veronica has got a bedroom in her house. In the bedroom there is a bed, a wardrobe, a desk and a chair. 5 There isn't a carpet and there isn't a television.

Skills Test 5&6
Exercise 1
A: 1 c 2 a 3 b 4 c 5 c
B: 1 a 2 c 3 a 4 b 5 b

Exercise 2
A: 1 T 2 F 3 T 4 F 5 T
B: 1 T 2 F 3 T 4 T 5 F

Exercise 3
A: 1 The guitar. 2 It's at four o'clock. 3 It's not a good idea. 4 I agree. 5 It's quarter to seven.
B: 1 I'm not sure. 2 It's half past two. 3 I agree. 4 He can act. 5 It's at eight o'clock.

Exercise 4
A: 1 no 2 no 3 yes 4 yes 5 no
B: 1 no 2 no 3 yes 4 yes 5 no

Exercise 5
A: 1 August 2 often 3 reads 4 writes 5 listens
B: 1 July 2 usually 3 listens 4 reads 5 writes

Exercise 6
Model text

> 1 He has a music lesson at quarter past three on Tuesdays. 2 He goes to Art Club at five o'clock on Wednesdays. 3 He plays football with his friends at half past four on Thursdays. 4 He has dinner with his family at quarter to seven on Fridays. 5 He hangs out with his friends in the park on Saturdays.

Skills Test 7&8
Exercise 1
A: 1 e 2 a 3 f 4 d 5 c
B: 1 c 2 f 3 a 4 g 5 e

Exercise 2
A: 1 T 2 T 3 T 4 F 5 F
B: 1 F 2 F 3 T 4 T 5 F

Exercise 3
A: 1 please 2 you are 3 here are 4 snowy 5 Whose
B: 1 have 2 That's 3 you are 4 like 5 Where

Exercise 4
A: 1 windsurfing 2 skiing 3 dangerous 4 hot 5 five
B: 1 beach 2 sailing 3 mountains 4 horse-riding 5 cold

Exercise 5
A: 1 going 2 brushes 3 vegetables 4 them 5 doesn't
B: 1 brushes 2 eating 3 them 4 drinks 5 does

Exercise 6
Model text

> 1 It's white and brown. 2 It eats vegetables and dog food. 3 It can do tricks. 4 It's clever and playful. 5 It likes playing with people and sleeping.

Mid-Year Test 1–4
Exercise 1
A: 1 France 2 spiky 3 eyes 4 clever 5 at
B: 1 Poland 2 wavy 3 eyes 4 funny 5 at

Exercise 2
A: 1 kitchen 2 living 3 console 4 in front of 5 window
B: 1 living 2 mobile 3 in front of 4 plant 5 kitchen

Exercise 3
A: 1 1 toes 2 tracksuit 3 cousin 4 cool 5 shoes
B: 1 cousin 2 toes 3 hoodie 4 boots 5 boring

Exercise 4
A: 1 a 2 b 3 d 4 e 5 c
B: 1 a 2 e 3 c 4 d 5 b

Exercise 5
A: 1 c 2 b 3 b 4 c 5 a
B: 1 c 2 b 3 a 4 b 5 c

Exercise 6
A: 1 Its 2 Her 3 Their 4 they 5 We
B: 1 Its 2 Your 3 We 4 they 6 Their

Exercise 7
A: 1 14 / fourteen 2 dark 3 6 / six 4 long 5 brown 6 11 / eleven
B: 1 14 / fourteen 2 spiky 3 6 / six 4 wavy/brown 5 brown/wavy 6 11 / eleven

Exercise 8
A: 1 What's 'lustro' in English? 2 Hello, Kevin. Nice to meet you. 3 Where are you from? 4 Where's the bathroom, please? 5 Sorry, my mistake. 6 Can you help me, please? 7 Would you like a sweet? 8 Who's your favourite actor?
B: 1 Hello, Adam. Nice to meet you. 2 Sorry, about that. 3 What's 'ołówek' in English? 4 Can you help me? 5 Where is she from? 6 Where's the bathroom, please? 7 Where's my coat? 8 What's your favourite film?

Exercise 9
A: 1 There's a garden (in front of the house). 2 It's next to the house. 3 Yes, he has. 4 There are three bedrooms (in the house). 5 No, it isn't. 6 It's in the kitchen.
B: 1 It's next to the sea. 2 A garage is next to the house. 3 Yes, he has. 4 There are three bedrooms (in the house). 5 There is one big room (in the house). 6 It's in the kitchen.

End-of-Year Test 1–8
Exercise 1
A: 1 snake 2 Monday 3 sailing 4 garden 5 neck
B: 1 tortoise 2 Friday 3 badminton 4 garden 5 head

Exercise 2
A: 1 sporty 2 does 3 walls 4 rabbit 5 fast
B: 1 sporty 2 does 3 door 4 hamster 5 fast

Exercise 3
A: 1 on 2 early 3 drink 4 out 5 guitar
B: 1 on 2 early 3 eat 4 hang 5 guitar

Exercise 4
A: 1 our 2 them 3 those 4 Ewa's 5 any
B: 1 this 2 them 3 our 4 a 5 Joe's

Exercise 5
A: 1 never goes 2 sitting 3 doesn't like 4 hasn't got 5 walking
B: 1 always goes 2 sitting 3 doesn't like 4 hasn't got 5 running

Exercise 6
A: 1 Is there (a rat under the table?) 2 Does (your mum) cook (for the family?) 3 (Where) do her grandparents (live?) 4 (Whose) mountain bike is (it?) 5 Can you play (golf?)
B: 1 Does (your dad) cook (for the family?) 2 (Whose) games console is it? 3 Can you play (hockey?) 4 (Where) do their cousins (live?) 5 Is there a skateboard in the wardrobe?)

Exercise 7
A: 1 six 2 Yes, (he is) 3 hockey 4 Yes, (she does) 5 animals 6 can't sing
B: 1 half past seven 2 school 3 Yes, (he can) 4 Yes, (she is) 5 write stories 6 actor

Exercise 8
A: 1 come 2 this 3 too 4 Let 5 about 6 Would 7 Let's 8 like
B: 1 Would 2 too 3 come 4 about 5 this 6 show 7 When 8 What's

Exercise 9
A: 1 T 2 T 3 T 4 F 5 DS 6 F
B: 1 T 2 F 3 T 4 DS 5 T 6 F